MOTIVATION AND RACING TACTICS
IN
TRACK AND FIELD

W. Harold "Skip" O'Connor

MOTIVATION AND RACING TACTICS
IN
TRACK AND FIELD

Parker Publishing Company, Inc. West Nyack, N.Y.

PRINTED IN THE UNITED STATES OF AMERICA

13-604066-7 BC

DEDICATED TO:

All of the fine athletes whose faith in me as
a coach helped me to become a better one.

FOREWORD

I HAVE BEEN ASSOCIATED WITH W. HAROLD "SKIP" O'CONNOR in track and field for many years. I have found him knowledgeable and scientific in his approach to coaching and am confident that this book will be another of his fine contributions to the literature on track and field.

THOMAS DUFFY
Track Coach
Holy Cross College
Worcester, Massachusetts

THE COACH,
THE RUNNER,
AND MOTIVATION

As RECORDS IN TRACK EVENTS EDGE LOWER AND LOWER and records in field events creep higher and higher, today's track coach and track athletes are faced with ever-increasing demands upon skill and dedication. Both the skill of the athlete and the skill of the coach are being tested to limits beyond anyone's expectations in even the recent past. A few years ago, the track man who dreamed of greatness in the mile could think in terms of a 4:10 mile. The prospective record holder in the shot put could set his sights on 60 feet, confident that if he reached it, he would rank with the finest. The sprinter could aim for a 9.4 in the 100-yard run with the assurance that this time would bring him world-wide recognition. The pole vaulter could set a goal of 16 feet, knowing well that such a height would place him among the elite of track.

How different are the prospects today! The runner's 4:10 mile would leave him trailing many a high school boy. The 60-foot shot putter would find himself overshadowed by dozens of men. The 9.4 sprinter would hardly raise an eyebrow in top competition. The 16-foot pole vaulter would find himself beaten frequently. Name any event in track and field and you will see records that make you gasp. Start at the top with the world records and go down the scale. At every level you will find marks that emphasize more clearly than words what it takes to reach the top today. In the words of both coach and athlete, "Things are getting tough all over."

Strangely enough, however, as runners whittle away the tenths of sec-

9

onds from records and add the inches to distances and heights, athletes keep trying and coaches keep learning till what seems to be the ultimate draws closer and closer. So, too, does the question, how can the athlete be motivated to meet the challenge, to face the sacrifices, and to approach the perfection of technique necessary. There must be self motivation by the athlete and inspirational motivation by the coach. More and more investigations are being made of the mechanics and skills involved in events, but in the last analysis, we are working with human beings, not with machines. True, there are problems of leverage, of applied force, of angles of release, and of stored energy. But man has always somehow managed to confound the scientific experts by achieving what appears impossible. It is by no means the purpose of this book to belittle the skills and techniques necessary for success in track and field, but rather to touch upon the inspirational and motivational aspects of the sport, to suggest tactics of competition, to make the athlete believe in himself; indeed, to rise above himself to reach goals which seemed almost nebulous.

Packed into this book, you will find a little of what Ken Doherty in his book *Modern Training for Running* calls *holism* in training, a little of Dr. Hans Selye's theory on stress, and a lot of plain old "Skip O'Connor" psychology and racing tactics that have led boys to performances well beyond their dreams.

Many of the suggestions in this book are based upon the writer's belief that the type of motivation valuable in one event is not necessarily the best type for a man competing in another. I mean by this that the problem faced by a sprinter, hurdler, or shot putter is not the same as that faced by a distance runner. The former must be keyed to short, explosive effort while the latter must be prepared to accept stress, even pain, for several minutes. He has to be motivated to continue in spite of distress and pain, while knowing that he can get immediate relief by slowing down or stopping. It becomes the coach's problem therefore to motivate the athlete to accept pain. This book will attempt to help the coach to suggest ways of motivating for both types of events.

We have ample proof that there are means of mass motivation that are effective and that these differ in some ways from those used in motivating the individual. This book proposes to treat such motivational tactics as they apply to the preparation of the team for team efforts. At the same time, we realize that the motivation of individuals for top effort involves quite different problems. Each man, devoted though he may be to team effort, still competes as an individual. He enters his event, keyed up by what will influence him as an individual. This drive may run the gamut all the way from fear to fame. Here again the writer offers a tip of the hat to that astute student of track and tracksters, Ken Doherty, for the insight evident in his urging of holism in the coaching of track athletes.

Just as we should recognize important differences between the motivation of teams and the motivation of individual athletes on these teams, so too should we recognize the difference in motivation necessary to stimulate the winning team toward a defense of its record and that needed to lift a losing team to the big effort to break that losing streak. The winner has many things going for him that the loser lacks. This book will offer suggestions for the motivation and racing tactics to be used with winning teams, but it will also have much to say about how the coach can motivate the team caught in the discouragement of a long losing streak. As a coach, the writer has known both the pleasure of the one and the frustration of the other.

I am convinced too that there is more than the nature of the athlete entering into the motivation. There is also the nature of the coach. I am aware that the tactics that I might use successfully could prove a flat failure with you. It is with this very thought in mind that I will be offering suggestions for *your* motivation of *your* athletes. Coming from some coaches, the "How are you, Champ?" approach of Dean Cromwell to his athletes would be a joke, effective though it was for Cromwell. This book proposes to take a look at you as a coach and the approaches that suit your personality and could be used without making you sound ridiculous and out of character.

I have been fortunate in my coaching career in having had many times the pleasant but challenging job of trying to motivate fine athletes for record-breaking attempts. There are many facets to this task, some of them quite subtle and difficult to manage. This book will treat the motivation of the boy who is "shooting for the record." I hope that some of the answers that I found will be the answers for you.

Though this book will concern itself with various training schedules and training methods, they will be introduced for their motivational aspects rather than as suggested training plans. Some consideration will be given to interval time averaging for distance runners, a device that Bob Timmons, the coach of Jim Ryun, Archie San Romani, Jr., and other fine distance runners, swears by. The samplings of workouts will be offered with analysis of their value in group motivation and their possibilities for individuals. Here you will learn something about the all-important question of *how they run,* but something too about *why they run* what they do run. And, of even more importance to you as a coach, you will find some suggestions of how your own athletes should run. Some evidence will be offered to show you that how your athletes run depends greatly upon how they believe they can run.

It is my belief that what leading educators have discovered about the value of audio-visual aids in classroom teaching has just as great an application to the track athlete. Many a boy misunderstands repeated *oral* correction of weaknesses but responds very quickly to what he sees revealed in a picture or movie of himself in action. The use of slides, personal sequence shots, and movies as motivational coaching devices will be discussed here.

Finally, you will find in this book some careful consideration of competitive tactics. Though some coaches may argue that pre-race plans are often upset, others are quick to point out that they quite often succeed. Here you will find discussion from which you may be able to draw conclusions.

"Skip" O'Connor

CONTENTS

Part I: INDIVIDUAL MOTIVATION

1.   Motivating and Working with Sprinters   19

Mind and Body Control in Starting, 27.   The Readiness for Starting, 29.   Timing the Starter, 29.   Reacting to the Gun Jumper, 29.   The Psychology of the Extra Lift, 33.   Timing the Drive for the Tape, 36.   Finishing Tactics, 37.   Coming Back After a Muscle Pull, 40.

2.   The Special Challenge in Developing Hurdlers   43

Working to Overcome Novice's Fear, 45.   Handling the Boy Who Balks, 46.   Spend Time on One Hurdle, 47.   Flexibility Exercises Aid Two Ways, 48.   Correcting the Hurdle Jumper, 48. Building Confidence for the Three Steps, 49.   Handling the Problem of Wind Conditions, 53.   Over-Distance Hurdling, 54. Working the Low Hurdler, 55.   Running the Intermediate Hurdles, 56.   Keying on the Head Position, 59.

3.   Coaching and Stimulating Middle Distance and Distance Runners   60

Motivating the Beginner, 60.   Motivation and Racing Tactics for the Quarter Miler, 61.   Developing Mediocre Talent, 62.   Stimulating the Star, 63.   The Dangers of Stress, 64.   Racing Tactics in the 440-Yard Run, 64.   Special Considerations, 65. Motivating and Planning Tactics for Half Milers, 66.   Racing Tactics in the 880, 70.   Working with Distance Runners, 72. Racing Tactics for Distance Runners, 85.   When the Lead Is Valuable in Distance Racing, 87.

4.   Motivation and Tactics in Relay Racing   88

Individual and Team Effort Involved, 88.   Working for Coordination, 89.   The Use of the Alternate, 90.   Placing Men for Effect, 96.   Using the "Take Charge" Man, 98.   Preparing for the Distance and Medley Relays, 100.   Putting Pressure on Opponents, 102.

5.   Working with Self-Driving Weight Men   105

Handling the Implements Correctly, 105.   Concentration of Effort in Fractional Time, 106.   The Build-Up of Implement Speed, 107.   Securing Controlled Speed, 108.   The Problem of Balance, 109.   What Fouling Reveals, 112.   Handling Individual's Tensions, 114.   The Psychology of Comfort, 117.   Coaching the Javelin Throwers, 117.   Using Weight Training as Motivation, 123.

6.   Building the Confidence of Jumpers   126

A Look at High Jumping, 126.   Developing Confidence, 127. The Importance of the Approach, 127.   Some Thoughts About Take-Off, 129.   Preparing for Difficulties, 131.   Creating Tension in Opponents, 131.   Coaching Help for Long Jumpers, 134. The Relationship of Speed to Long Jumping, 134.   Getting Height Off the Board, 135.   The Importance of the Landing, 137.

7.   Coaching the Fibre Glass Pole Vaulter   139

Correcting Fallacies, 142.   Creating Confidence for the Wait, 142. Noticing the Direction of Pole Bend, 143.   The Rock Back, 144. Wind Conditions Relating to the Approach, 145.   Placing the Uprights, 145.   The Matching of Pole and Vaulter, 146. Weight Training Is Valuable, 146.

8.   Working with the Prospective Record Breaker   150

The Importance of Individual Attention, 150.   The Star as a Team Aid, 151.   Using the Status Symbol, 151.   The Significance of "Inner Drive," 153.   Planning the Attacks of the Record, 153.   Checking and Using the Opposition, 154.   Playing up the Athlete's Strengths, 154.   Tension and the Outstanding Athlete, 155.   Considerations for the Future, 155.

Part II: TEAM MOTIVATION

9.   Preparation for Adverse Conditions   159

The Value of Modern Investigations, 159.   Ordinary Precautions Are Not Enough, 161.   Some Thoughts About Varying Approaches, 162.   Practicing in the Rain, 162.   Hurdling Against a Strong Wind, 164.   Planning Relay Passes for Problem Areas, 165.   Planning for Indoor Racing Conditions, 165.   Some Seeming Trivia, 166.

10.   Meeting the Opponent's Psychology   169

Respect Your Opponent's Ability, 170.   Some Fear Is Not Folly, 171.   Racing Strategy as Motivation, 171.   Faith in One's Own Ability, 173.   Tactics in Early Stages of the Events, 173.

11.   Prepping the Team for a Championship   175

"Winning on Paper," 176.   The Psychology of Anticipation, 176. The Value of Early Planning, 177.   Possibilities of Improvement in Events, 178.   Possible Improvement in Hurdles, 178.   Sprinters Show Limited Improvement, 179.   Improvement of Distance Runners, 179.   Consider Packing a Weak Event, 181.   Let Some Events Alone, 181.   Consider the Importance of Seeding, 181.   The Significance of Seedings, 182.   Making Use of Meet Rules, 183.   Preparing the Athlete for the Extended Meet, 184.

12.   Breaking the Losing Streak   187

The Problem of New Morale, 187.   Assessing Your Team's Chances, 188.   Planning the Workouts, 189.   Hiding Your Strength, 190.   Stimulating the Team for the Big Effort, 191. Discussing the Meet Tactics, 193.

13.   Preparing for Special Events   196

Working with Beginning Triple Jumpers, 197.   Starting Work with Hammer Throwers, 204.   Some Thoughts About the Steeplechase, 208.   Preparing the Decathlon Man, 211.

Index   215

Part I
Individual Motivation

MOTIVATING AND
Chapter 1 | WORKING WITH SPRINTERS

When a track coach faces a group of prospective sprinters for the first time, the thoughts running through his mind are probably not too different from those that he has when he faces any group of candidates for any track event. He is probably asking himself, "What differences in potential have I here?" His next inward question may be, "How far can I develop such potential?" If he is a good coach, he probably will know some of the answers from experience. He will know that the boy who runs a 12-second hundred yards has been limited by nature far more than the boy of the same age who without training runs the same distance in 11 seconds. Let's assume, however, that a third boy in the group covers the distance in 10.6. The high school coach who sees the third candidate probably looks up with a gleam in his eye and says to himself, "Ah, I've got a sprinter." If another boy in the group approaches 10 seconds for the distance, the coach bubbles over a little more and with great glee assures himself, "Brother, I've got a *star!*"

Now certainly there isn't anything earth-shattering or even really surprising in the preceding comments. We are talking merely of the recognition of potential, and it doesn't take much track knowledge to spot the difference between the 12-second man and the 10-second man. Yet the very differences in potential lead the good coach to speculation about the second question. Many a coach has pondered long over the possibility of making the 12-second sprinter into a 10-second man. Over and over again coaches have insisted that sprint talent is God-given and that there is very little a coach can do to make sprinters out of boys who show little potential. Like many another coach, I have long noted that a Bob Hayes, a Tommy Smith, or a Jesse Owens stood out in high school just as obviously as he did in the Olympics or the National Intercollegiates. But the gnawing questions always remain, how far can we develop the talent we see before us? Can we do more with strength development? Can we bring the sprinter along farther with more stretching, more starts, more short sprints, or more plain hard work? Most of all, we ask ourselves, is it a fact that sprinters are born, or are we still awaiting the day when the secret of sprint talent will be revealed and some evidence will prove to us that a sprinter can be made.

Perhaps we should begin our consideration of the motivation of sprinters with a look at the part that natural talent plays and follow this with a study of how much improvement it is reasonable to expect. Though we may joke about the impossible being just a little harder to accomplish, we know in our hearts that there are limits to what a sprinter can do, regardless of excellence of motivation. One of our real problems is to find out from the available evidence what those limits are. We may be confident that the 9-second 100 yards will soon be run, just as surely as the 4-minute mile was run. But are we as ready to believe that an 8-second 100 yards may some day be the goal toward which some coach will be driving his superstar?

When we think of the high school sprinter are we being unreasonable in setting a goal of 9 seconds for the hundred when the boy is a star? Before we laugh off such a possibility, we need to take a long look at that 9.3 hundred run by Billy Gaines, the New Jersey schoolboy sensation. We need to notice that he was only a high school junior when he ran that awesome century. Perhaps we should also consider the youthfulness of sprint champions at their peak in comparison with the maturity of distance runners at theirs. It is no great track secret that the loss of speed becomes a factor early in any athlete's life. Should we as coaches not be giving some thought to our very young but very great swimming stars and perhaps seeing in them a clue to the possibilities of our high school sprinters?

Long ago Fred Wilt, a very astute and dedicated track man and track coach, insisted that track men are *always* far short of their potential. I think that Fred is absolutely right in this. I am firmly convinced that sprinters who think that they are going their fastest really *are not*. I contend that this is just as true of the mediocre sprinters as of the super-stars. The boy with the limited talent may well be using even less of that talent than the star with the seemingly limitless speed. But I believe that we coaches should not be so awed by the star's speed that we overlook the fact that he too is falling short of his potential.

When we begin our motivation of our sprinters, we need to do so firm in our conviction that not one of them is reaching more than 80 percent of his possible speed and that many of them are below that. This is to say that obviously we are still far from the ultimate in sprinting. What this means to you as a coach is that you have more chance of improving any sprinter you have than you might think. I am not for a minute saying here that sprinters can be made of anyone and everyone. Natural speed still makes the sprinter stand out among his fellows. Fortunately for us coaches, it shows up very early, even in the boy's childhood. What I am really pointing out is that it may not be unreasonable to assume that the 11-second high school junior may become the 10-second high school senior though he may never become the 9-second dash man. The 10-second junior may become the 9-second senior. Before we go completely overboard with this thinking we should refer again to the contention that track men seldom use more than 70 to 80 percent of their talent. What we are saying by this is that *they are running at four-fifths speed.*

We may look at some of our outstanding sprint stars and find this assertion hard to believe. It seems difficult to accept the thought that a Billy Gaines or a Tommy Smith or a Bob Hayes could be running at less than top speed. Yet we have only to recall certain outstanding efforts by these same sprinters to find that on given days they suddenly turned in times two or three tenths of a second faster than ever before. We need to think back to certain races against outstanding opponents in which at given points these same stars found *that little extra* at the very time that they *seemed* to be going at top speed. This is not to discount the possibility of better starts, though these too must be a part in our motivation and preparation of our next generation of sprinters. What I am referring to is the obvious lift in the final stages of the race. The effort that produced that little extra speed proved that the extra speed *was there to be used.*

One of the biggest sprint races of recent years saw Charlie Greene of Nebraska meeting head on with Jim Hines and Canada's Harry Jerome. In that race under admittedly fine racing conditions, Greene was beaten in 10 seconds flat for the 100 meters. Yet only a few days later Charlie turned in a world's record equalling 9.1 for the 100 yards. Even assuming a better start in the record-tying race, we have to admit that in the earlier race against Hines of Texas Southern and Jerome of Canada, Greene could not have been going his fastest. The tension evident in his face and his subsequent fall flat on the track at the finish made it obvious that Greene was losing speed in his effort to gain it. Indeed there remains the nagging thought that neither Greene in his 9.1 century nor Hines in his 10-second 100 meters had been going his fastest. This Hines proved with his 9.9 in Mexico City.

When we consider the regularity with which sprinters have been running 9.1 in the 100 yards recently, we have to consider seriously the possibility that our sprinters have been hitting only about 80 percent of their potential.

One of the most frequent comments heard from any group of coaches watching a sprinter in a record-breaking performance is, "He ran easily. If some one had been pushing him, he might have gone even faster." If you had talked with the sprinter himself after his great race, you would have been very likely to get a comment like this: "I felt nice and loose. I am sure that I could have gone faster if I had to." Here we have further indication from both coaches and athlete that even in a record-breaking performance there did not seem to be full use of potential.

Yet it is this very impression of "something held back" that may mislead both coach and athlete. The coach in an effort to drive his sprinter faster and faster must not overlook the part that relaxation itself played in the successful effort. It was the relaxation that made the race seem effortless. The coach who then tries to get greater speed from his sprinter by demanding greater effort may well be thinking in terms of what *looks* like all-out effort. He may be visualizing the agonizing strain of facial muscles that seems to be associated with an athlete's giving to his fullest. Herein lies the danger of mismotivation. It is quite possible that in his next race, the sprinter, following his coach's suggestion and even his own impression drawn from the successful effort earlier, may make a *visibly* greater effort but with disappointing results. It is quite probable that his time in the second race will be slower than that of the first. (See Figures 1a and 1b.)

Figure 1a

STRAIN—HIGH SCHOOL SPRINTERS.

Figure 1b

STRAIN—HIGH SCHOOL SPRINTERS.

Here we seem to have a paradox. The sprinter in his record-breaking performance is actually not going his fastest; yet when the coach prods him into greater effort the result is disappointing. The runner, who felt at the time of the record-breaking race that he was not going his fastest, finds that if he tries harder, he is slower. Something seems amiss. What then must coach and sprinter do to bring the sprinter to full achievement of his potential? (See Figure 2.)

Figure 2

RELAXATION—CARTER OF DANVERS HIGH SCHOOL.

Photo by Lou LaPrade, Falmouth, Mass.

First of all, it may be wise to recall that in his relaxed race the sprinter sensed his latent speed and strength. Yet the stress and strain, the facial contortions, the tight, flailing arms, are the things he remembers when he insists later, "I couldn't go any faster. I went all out." Isn't it strange that in his highly successful effort his impression was, "I could have gone faster"? Consider a great performance by any athlete in any sport. The loose, relaxed fielder makes the great play look easy in baseball. The great fighter hits a stunning jab in a motion like the flick of a snake's tongue. The loose, easy flip of the wrists gets the soft basketball shot away before the man guarding the shooter can prevent it. There can be little argument that the relaxed muscle moves faster than the tense one. How then can we motivate the sprinter to relax?

Some coaches have advocated training for flexibility. What part can flexibility exercises play in improving the speed of sprinters? If sprint speed cannot be taught, in what areas do we work to improve our sprinter's ability to use the talent that he has? Will improvement of ankle flexibility, for example, enable a sprinter to use more efficiently the speed that he has? Nationally known coaches like Bud Winter have done considerable work in this area. His coaching film on sprinting put out by the Frank Ryan Enterprises shows definite effort to increase ankle flexibility.[1]

At first glance, it would seem reasonable that flexibility training by freeing the joints would contribute to increased speed. Yet Dr. George B. Dintiman of Inter American University of Puerto Rico in an article in *Scholastic Coach* titled "Increasing Running Speed," contended after extensive research that, "an increase in hip and ankle flexibility has no apparent effect upon running speed as measured by the 50-yard dash." He added that, "a flexibility training program used as a supplement to sprint training didn't improve speed significantly more than an unsupplemented sprint-training program."[2]

Dr. Dintiman's research did, however, lead to the conclusion that *a combination* of both weight training and flexibility training used to supplement sprint training has been shown to increase running speed in the 50-yard dash significantly more than an unsupplemented sprint-training program.[3]

It would seem to me that while some coaches might wonder about these conclusions they do have the backing of careful research and might

[1] *Sprinting with Bud Winter* (Film), New Haven, Conn.: Frank Ryan Enterprises.

[2] George B. Dinteman, "Increasing Running Speed" *Scholastic Coach* (March, 1965) p. 58.

[3] Dinteman, "Increasing Running Speed" *Scholastic Coach* (March, 1965) p. 58.

be utilized in preparing and motivating sprinters more sensibly than hit-or-miss methods. If the coach is to motivate his sprinter effectively, he must be able to convince the athlete that his training suggestions do work. The reliance upon flexibility exercises without weight training could prove disappointing. Certainly until more evidence can be offered, such findings as Dr. Dintiman's must be considered.

This leads us now to the question of what part weight training should play in the development and motivation of sprinters. The question is raised frequently as to whether or not to use weight training at all as a supplement to sprint training. Many coaches insist on it; some reject it. Another question frequently raised is whether to use heavy weights with few repetitions or light weights with more and faster repetitions. Some coaches ask, "Will the development of the arm and upper body strength really produce significant increases in running speed?" Others question, "Can weight training actually have a detrimental effect on body flexibility?" Another question asked is, "How often should I encourage my sprinters to do weight training?"

In attempting to answer such questions, I feel that some knowledge of the laws of motion is important to the coach if he is to make reliable decisions about the training and motivation of runners. One of the finest sources of information on body mechanics available is Geoffrey Dyson's *The Mechanics of Athletics.*[4] But for our purposes here, perhaps we should pay close attention to what is known as Newton's Second Law, "The acceleration of a body is proportional to the force causing it." Now, we know that the ability of a man to apply force depends not only upon speed but also upon strength. The sprinter's reaction time is involved in the speed with which he applies force to the blocks at the instant the gun is fired. But the length of time that he applies the force and the strength with which he applies it are also factors. This is just as true of the force he applies to the ground in each stride. Thus it seems reasonable to assume that increased strength can contribute to the more efficient use of speed. In other words, if the force applied by the sprinter at the point of application, whether this be the blocks or the ground itself, can be increased, the acceleration of the sprinter should improve. Thus weight training that increases leg strength should be helpful to the sprinter, and the coach in using a weight training program judiciously should soon have evidence of the improvement. The recognition of success is bound to give the athlete confidence in his coach and serve as effective motivation.

In attempting to motivate his sprinters toward maximum effort, the

---

[4] Geoffrey Dyson, *The Mechanics of Athletics*, New York, N.Y.: Dover Publications, Inc.

coach will often have to contend with pre-conceived notions of the effects of weight training upon the flexibility of joints. Even though the coach may be convinced that the use of heavy weights is beneficial to the development of strength in sprinters, he may find his athletes reluctant to accept the use of heavy weights, claiming that the gain in strength is offset by the loss of flexibility. Actually there is no concrete evidence that this is true, but since we are dealing here with the motivation of the athlete, we must consider the sprinter's attitude.

Many coaches themselves are still not convinced that the use of heavy weights involving slow lifts and few repetitions is better for sprinters than the use of light weights with fast lifts and more repetitions. I am not one who has the notion that the use of heavy weights with slow lifts can restrict the flexibility of the runner, but I believe that the coach will find acceptance of the light weights with fast lifts easier to get from sprinters. First of all, such a lifting program is more in line with the ideas that the sprinter has about his particular event. He pictures himself acting and reacting with speed, and the heavy weight-slow lift series seems unrelated. We have to be realistic about this in our coaching. In the final analysis, the athlete is motivated by what *he* believes, not by what *we* believe. Let me assure you that I am not about to suggest that you forget weight training for sprinters. Nothing could be farther from my mind. I want to point out, however, that the development of muscular endurance through training with light weights and fast lifts not only aids that endurance but contributes to muscle strength as well. My feeling is that two purposes can be served by advocating such a program. First, though it may take longer for the athlete to gain local muscular strength using the lighter weights, it will achieve the same end, provided enough resistance is involved in the lifts, and along with the more gradual increase in strength, it will aid muscular endurance. The latter is a factor in all sprints, even the 100-yard dash. It is even more a factor in the 220 and 440. Secondly, I feel that with schoolboys, and with some college men too, the danger of injury through *misus*e of heavy weights can be avoided.

One aspect of a weight training program, it seems to me, should receive far more attention than it now does. I refer to the use of light dumbbells in the runner's hands as he moves his arms rapidly in correct running form. I believe that the exercise has even more benefit if used by the sprinter while running in place. The use of a 5-pound dumbbell in each hand as the sprinter simulates the rapid arm action of sprinting in place will not only help to strengthen the arms but aid in flexibility as well. It may be well for the coach to consider the use of weighted implements in the warm-up of athletes in other sports. Any track coach who has ever played golf knows the effect of swinging a weighted club or a pair of clubs before he hits from the first tee. The driver feels unusually light to him as he swings it. The hitter going to the on-deck circle in baseball and even on the way to the plate is seldom seen not swinging his two bats or some sort of weighted club. Knowing the feelings of the golfer and the hitter, I suggest that we coaches in track may be missing a bet in not trying the same method with our sprinters. Why not have a sprinter just before his call to the marks use light weights while driving his arms rapidly. The psychological lift that results as he takes off with the gun can well be added motivation for him. Certainly the feeling of lightness of arms and looseness of the upper body can add to the confidence of the sprinter in his ability to get faster arm action in the start and in the early stages of his race.

You will note that I refer again and again to methods by which I hope that we coaches can influence our sprinters to give more than that 80 percent effort in a race. Having emphasized how much of the sprinter's misconception of his going at full speed is mental rather than physical, I am hammering away at anything and everything that can set his mind at ease, aid his flexibility, and add to his strength so that a maximum effort will be the result.

MIND AND BODY CONTROL IN STARTING

Since so little can be done about the sprinter's natural speed, coaches have worked increasingly on his starting. There can be no doubt that reaction times can be improved, block placement can be made more efficient and balance can be corrected for more effective racing. It is not the purpose of this writer, however, to debate the methods of starting or the placement of starting blocks except as these factors may or may not have some value in the motivation of the sprinters. In a limited way, practically anything that a sprinter does successfully can motivate him positively, provided he is conscious of it. If he has confidence in his block placement, he may get a better start even though such placement may not be the most mechanically efficient. Whether the sprinter should use the bunch start, the medium start, or the elongated start, or a variation of any one of them suited to him, may be debatable. It seems to me that starting position in the sprints is a highly individual thing; it may well be that the complication of the human body is such that our efforts to make it follow the strict laws of mechanics are thwarted by the very nature of the body. We coaches constantly criticize the efficiency of the starts of some of our best sprinters. Since we recognize the start as so important, what can we do to improve a sprinter's start? If we want relaxation, do we insist on a style of start that makes him feel ill at ease or do we accept the less efficient start that nevertheless makes him more confident of getting away fast? Are we oversimplifying when we try to apply the laws of mechanics directly to the human body? I raise this question fully aware that this may bring down the scorn of physicists who can point to theories and even laws of mechanics to support their contention that these apply just as truly to human beings as to machines. Yet I recall very vividly the errors made by such experts when they insisted that certain absolute limits for man existed in the pole vault, the dashes, and other events, only to see their predictions shattered wholesale as years went on. Remember that not too long ago the bunch start was supposedly proved by research to excel all others in getting the sprinter away from his blocks and into top speed. Later research, however, seems to prove that the sprinter using the bunch start gets off the blocks quickest but soon loses that momentum because of weakness in balance. The medium elongated start was then designated as the start that enabled the sprinter to accelerate fastest. You have only to study the block placement of the famous sprinters coached by Bud Winter to notice that he has departed even further from the once highly touted bunch start.

In our attempts to motivate our sprinters, should we insist on the type of start now in vogue or should we recognize the sprinter as an individual and work with him until we find the type of start that gives him the confidence that he needs? Here again, it seems to me that proper motivation of the sprinter may be far more beneficial to him than any fixed idea of exact angle of leverage. Don't misunderstand. I am not attacking the efficiency of accepted starting methods. I am merely pointing out that if the bunch start gives your sprinter more confidence than the elongated start, you must decide whether he will gain more from such confidence than he may lose through the tiny difference possible in starting efficiency now claimed for the bunch start. You must decide whether you will follow the advocates of mechanical perfection in starting or those who see starting as a very individual matter. Certainly we must correct obvious flagrant errors in starting, but we may need more study of a newer science, that of *human motion*.

I would even go so far as to say that if your sprinter is plagued by lack of speed off the blocks, you may be wise to revert to the bunch start, the one that gets him away fastest. If he can move off the blocks in good balance, he may find this advantage more than offsetting the slight loss in acceleration that science now tells us results from the bunch start. If by using the bunch start, as many of our top sprinters still do, you can give your sprinter the confidence that results in his extending himself nearer to his limit, who can say that you are wrong? We coaches are still dealing with men, not with machines.

THE READINESS FOR STARTING

Watch any group of sprinters on their marks awaiting the starter's gun and you are bound to notice many weaknesses in technique, but you will be lax indeed if you fail to notice the signs of tension that show vividly in many little ways even in our finest sprinters. The villain at work here is *fear*. Though not in the degree that shows when one is in great danger, it is nevertheless fear in subtle form. The chronic gun jumper is actually moved by fear of being caught on his marks. He is motivated by an urge to beat the gun, get that little advantage that will help him avoid the even greater fear of defeat. He is tense and over-anxious. The sprinter frequently caught on his marks at the gun is a different problem. He is listening, *listening for the gun*. He doesn't move until after the gun sounds. Then we have the sprinter drawn off his marks by the gun jumper. The fact is that this boy may well be closer to ideal starting technique than you imagine. What draws him off his mark? Perhaps it is the *flash of color* he sees out of the corner of his eye as the gun jumper moves. Perhaps it is the *sound* of the gun jumper's movement.

TIMING THE STARTER

What we are observing here is in one case reaction to visual stimulus and in the other, reaction to auditory stimulus. Perhaps in some cases we are seeing response to both. We know that some people react effectively to the visual while others react more swiftly to sound. It is quite possible that some coaches of future world's champion sprinters may find it worthwhile to study the man's response to both visual and auditory stimulus to determine which will set him off faster. The sprinter with good peripheral vision may one day be jockeying for a starting lane that will help him to catch the flash of the starter's gun. The man who moves faster through reaction to sound may be looking for the lane closest to the starter.

REACTING TO THE GUN JUMPER

It is my belief that the boy who is drawn off his marks by the gun jumper may be doing what I consider most important. He may be concentrating so intensely upon *GOING* that *any* sudden noise will *set him off*. I *want* him to concentrate on *just that, GOING*.

In conjecturing about a still distant future in which records in the sprints may have to be measured in hundredths of seconds instead of in tenths of seconds, we may not be far wrong in stressing every tiny aid to the sprinter. Indeed, every aid may be significant. I am convinced that such little points as response to visual or auditory stimulus will not be thought of as fantastic before the next 25 years pass.

Let's not entirely forget such possibilities, but let's turn for the present to the motivation of today's sprinter toward better starts. It seems to me that the greatest problem we coaches have to contend with today is the sprinter's *lack of concentration*. What he is thinking about in "Set" position may be his opponents, his block placement, the starter, his secret fears, or any of a dozen different things. What he *should* be thinking of exclusively is *GOING*. If he is concentrating on this alone, the starter's gun will set him off automatically. In fact, almost any unusual sound will set him in motion. You can prove this to yourself and to your athlete by making even so slight a sound as the snapping of your fingers. If he is poised and ready, he will go on the slightest sound.

When you are thinking in terms of motivation for better starts for your sprinter, it seems to me that you are working in reverse unless you are actually spending quite a bit of your time with him when he is practising from the blocks. If you expect the sprinter to improve off the marks, there seems to be little point in sending him off by himself to work. What he does while alone may have very little relationship to what you want him to do. I believe that almost all of us coaches are lax in this respect. It is very easy to say to the boy, "Go over to the blocks and take a half-dozen full speed starts." Even though I have done it myself occasionally, I still think it is a mistake.

I am convinced that improvement in starting will come only with the utmost concentration and effort of both athlete and coach. The sprinter must become accustomed to giving full attention to every start he takes, even in practice. I am not insistent that he start with a gun every time, but I want him to start with some sound that he can react to. He can't do this alone; he can do it only rather inefficiently with the aid of a teammate. If your sprinter's poor starting is what worries you, don't expect it to improve unless you make it seem important to the boy by being with him constantly when he practices starts.

If the sprinter is in the habit of rising sharply as the gun sounds, you can help him to get the feel of powerful forward drive by borrowing a trick from the football coaches. You can give your sprinter the feel of correct forward drive by placing your hands on his shoulders as he gets into set position and then bracing yourself as you have him try to drive you backward. Set your own body in such a position that you are in line with his legs as they drive him off the blocks. He should not be lifting you upward but actually driving you backward with the power of his thrust off the blocks. With a little practice you can find an angle of pressure that is nearly correct for each of your sprinters. A little work of this kind I have found helpful in developing the confidence of a sprinter in his ability to get maximum drive off the blocks. Of course, he must be taught not to make his thrust off the blocks a lunge that leaves him off balance. He must feel the power of his legs driving you several steps backward. Don't overdo the stunt, but don't be afraid to try it with a boy who is lifting his head and making his first motion upward instead of forward.

Another device that seems to me to be neglected in training sprinters to accelerate fast off the blocks is the *competitive 15-yard dash*. We expect our sprinters to be in full speed as soon as possible. This means that we hope that they can reach full speed in the first 40 yards of a 100-yard dash. It may seem to you that you should therefore be having them run intrasquad 40-yard dashes. For motivational purposes, however, I try to emphasize the importance of acceleration by urging the sprinters to try for maximum speed in the first 15 or 20 yards of the race. They really cannot achieve this, but they will get the message if you keep insisting, "This is a 15-yard dash. The finish line is here. You must come off the blocks running." I have found that sprinters enjoy this competitive practice. It is one of the best ways I know to drill into their minds the value of fine starting. There is no room for error. Even very good sprinters can find themselves beaten by lesser ones when they come off the blocks in poor balance or with poor forward drive, because the race is over before they can make up the fraction of a second that they lose by the mistake. So, if you really want to develop the sprinter's start, why not work on that phase of the race alone. What you are trying to get is full drive off the blocks with correct balance for rapid acceleration. Starts alone will give you only half the results you want. Motivate your sprinter's starting by forcing him to combine it with very rapid acceleration. Both factors are highly important, and for effective sprinting they must lead to full stride in the body of the race.

This brings us now to the phase of the race in which the athlete is presumably in full stride. According to the tests available to us, the athlete, even in as short a race as the 100-yard dash, can continue in full speed for a surprisingly short distance before actually beginning to lose speed, though in almost imperceptible amounts. As has been said before, the sprinter who accelerates to full speed fastest from the blocks and sustains that speed longest is likely to be the winner. Personally, I believe that this second phase has as much room for improvement as starting does. I am aware that some coaches, Bud Winter especially, have done quite a bit of work emphasizing the strong, flexible, relaxed stride in sprinting. I think that it is time that we coaches did much more work with the development of full stride sprinting. There is much to be done.

Some coaches have advocated the use of downhill sprinting at full speed as practice to force the sprinters to maximum leg extension. I must

Figure 3a

JOHN COLLINS OF HOLY CROSS COLLEGE WINNING 100 YARD DASH, NEW ENGLAND INTERCOLLEGIATE CHAMPIONSHIP.

Figure 3b

JOHN COLLINS NEARING FINISH OF NEW ENGLAND INTERCOLLEGIATE 220.

confess, however, that I have not been too enthusiastic about such a device. I am reluctant to use it because I feel that the sprinter builds up so much momentum that he is often completely off balance. I do not think that this lends itself to good sprinting. It is my contention that the sprinter must never be off balance if he is to achieve his maximum speed. I am opposed to over-extension of stride in any race and I am sure that it can work against a runner in any race, even as short a one as the dash. Note the accompanying photos to see what happens when a sprinter tries to extend his stride beyond what is natural for him (Figures 3a and 3b).

Since it is the task of every coach to motivate his sprinters to use what speed they have to best advantage, he must in the future spend more time helping the boy to achieve his real potential when in full stride. We coaches spend a great deal of time working on more efficient starts for one reason, *to get the sprinter into full stride as quickly as possible.* It seems rather silly then to spend so much time preparing the boy to reach full sprint stride and comparatively little time trying to help him sustain that speed with efficiency through the rest of the race.

THE PSYCHOLOGY OF THE EXTRA LIFT

To help your sprinter attain maximum speed, *not* what he may think is maximum speed, you must make him believe that he definitely can move faster. It is amazing what a man's belief in himself will do. I have long used a racing stimulus that I think brings results. Indeed, I have *seen* it bring results. I am sure that any coach will agree that what we want from the sprinter is a type of action that may be described as *vigorous but relaxed.* Any coach will agree that tension prevents the sprinter from such achievement. I contend that it is worthwhile to have the boy concentrate upon additional acceleration at a certain point in the dash. This conscious effort to get a "lift" about 20 or 25 yards from the finish serves two purposes. First, it spurs the sprinter to greater effort at a time when he thinks that he is going his fastest. Secondly, the sprinter is concentrating upon his planned move, not worrying about his opponent or about his own brief moment of pain. To me this seems good medicine. I know that some coaches raise the objection that the sprinter may hold back something, knowing that he is expected to drive from the special point to the finish. I try to prevent such a mistake by working upon that very thing during many practice sessions. In other words, I am looking for full speed *and then some.* When we coaches succeed in making our sprinters believe that they have untapped speed reserves, then we will be getting closer to drawing their full potential from them.

It would be wrong, however, to think that the mind of the athlete alone is the barrier between him and full speed. He must run with his body, or we should say with both mind and body. This means that we must coach better running action and help the sprinter to greater strength. Groups of muscles that are the main seats of tension trouble are in the abdomen, the shoulders, the face and neck, the hands and arms, and even in the legs. These are the areas of tension that we must work on so that the body will do its full share in reaching full speed. The boy who feels tight will be afraid to extend himself to the utmost. Always in his mind is the fear of the pulled muscle. Yet, ironically, that very fear may *lead* to the pull.

I confess that I have at times been reluctant to insist upon full speed sprinting. I have resorted to half speed and three-quarter speed work like many other coaches. In the back of my mind, however, there was always the nagging thought that what the boy did at three-quarter speed did not make the demands upon his body that full speed sprinting did, and that unless he moved at full speed his weaknesses would not really show. I do not mean to say that I would not resort to half speed or even slow motion to show and correct any serious error in form. I do mean that we coaches must have the sprinter do certain amounts of high speed sprinting in practice to learn to use his body efficiently under such speeds.

The coach who wants to develop his sprinter's confidence in his own ability to make extra demands upon his body in the dash must help him to eliminate the little builders of tension that result in the body tightness that stops him. By watching his sprinter's head, the coach can see important signs of trouble. Certainly the slight swaying of the head from side to side can be pointed out as waste motion detracting slightly from the full forward drive of the body. The coach can observe the tightening neck and facial muscles that show lack of relaxation. He can work with the sprinter to bring about the looseness that they both want. Strain that shows in tight arm muscles and clenched hands can also be worked on. Little by little, coach and athlete can work to lessen or eliminate such flaws in sprint action. This is why I sometimes had dash men sprinting at full speed for 120 yards. I was then able to see what effects the sustained sprinting effort would have upon the runner's form.

In attempting to induce your sprinters to go beyond what they now consider full speed, it is good to keep in mind certain points about the mechanics of sprinting. We should be looking for correct points to stress, not just flaws to criticize. In other words, we need to have in mind what *should* be done, not just what should *not* be done. It seems to me that our future great sprinters will have to be coached more positively than those of today.

Studies of running efficiency have shown rather conclusively that at full speed the runner's body angle should be approximately 70 degrees or about 20 degrees from the vertical. This means that when a sprinter is moving at full speed *efficiently*, we should see maximum extension of the legs driving the body forward at the correct angle. We need to remember that *a muscle is strongest under stretch*. To get the full leg extension that we want, we must look for the powerful thrust of the whole foot against the track. The sprinter's heel must touch, only for an instant, it is true, but it must touch so that maximum extension of the ankle and foot can be achieved. If you want to observe the importance of the big toe alone in the movement of a sprinter, notice how effectively an injury to the big toe will kill his speed. Flexibility exercises that enable the sprinter to use his leg strength down to the very tip of his big toe can thus be seen as valuable.

If you watch many sprinters carefully as they move at top speed, you are likely to observe more splay-footed action than you imagine. This means that such sprinters can be helped to move more efficiently by the coach's insistence that they try for full forward drive from the entire foot.

Your insistence on the drive forward from the whole foot is nothing more than the application of Newton's Third Law, "For every action there is always an opposite and equal reaction." The strength of the thrust can be diminished if the direction of it is not straight ahead. The duration of the force is involved in the use of the whole foot in the drive off the ground in each stride just as truly as it is in the drive off the starting blocks. If the sprinter is urged to place as much of his foot as possible against the blocks in starting, he certainly should be taught to get as much as possible of his foot in contact with the ground in each stride.

If you have not already studied Bud Winter's film on sprinting put out by the Frank Ryan Enterprises of New Haven, Connecticut, it will be well worth your while to see the types of practice that he uses with his sprinters to get ankle flexibility. It seems to me that the improvement of our future sprinters must involve the combination of such flexibility exercises and carefully planned strength building to bring talented sprinters to maximum efficiency.

Besides looking for a 70 degree body angle in the sprinter at full speed, we should be watching for high knee action—but not so high that it is bounce-producing. We should be insisting upon vigorous arm action, but with the arms and hands loose and relaxed. Facial muscles should also be relaxed. Perhaps I can best describe what I think we must get from our sprinters by saying, "He should learn to run with abandonment." He should feel as though his speed is unlimited. A talented and well prepared sprinter who can forget the fear of a pull will be the great one of tomorrow.

Still another consideration for our runners in the future, sprinters as well as distance men, or even for our field event men, is one that is seldom mentioned. We know that our bodies perform tasks more efficiently at certain times of the day than at others. We know too the time of day is not necessarily the same for one man as for another. We also know that a tired person will react more slowly than a rested one. This leads me to think that our future training schedules, when possible, should make use of this knowledge. Once we know the hours of the day during which a man performs best, we may be able to arrange practices for him during such times. At any rate we can give greater thought than we now do to this factor as it affects practice results. I realize that this means much individual work and attention, but I am convinced that we will need to make such concessions to get the results we will need to threaten future records.

Next we must give some thought to the finish of the dash. I am speaking here not of the final strides alone but of that phase of the dash beyond which the runner starts to lose top speed. In the 100-yard or 100-meter dash this is likely to be that part of the race beyond 80 yards. For some sprinters, it may be at 65 or 70 yards, depending upon how long they can maintain top speed after they reach it. Perhaps in the future we may find ways to train our sprinters to sustain top speed another ten or 20 yards, but until we do, we have to think of the last 25 yards or so as the finish phase of the 100.

TIMING THE DRIVE FOR THE TAPE

Let's study first the actions of the sprinter as he reaches that point in the dash at which his top speed begins to fall off, be it ever so slightly. It is at this precise moment that I think good motivation can pay off. This is the point at which I want that sprinter to forget his feelings, even if it be only for an instant, *to think of a planned move.* I want him, almost in spite of himself, to move faster. I can assure you that I have seen dramatic results from even ordinary high school sprinters who became convinced that they could go faster at this point. Since I consider the arms an important factor in good sprinting, I urge the athlete to keep his arms and hands loose but to try to drive them faster and faster as he approaches the finish line. Since the head leads the body, the sprinter should be urged to keep his neck muscles loose and his chin down while his eyes focus on a point a few yards ahead. Because I am asking the sprinter to sustain top speed for a longer time than usual, I realize that I am now stressing *endurance.* Strange though it may sound to some, it is true that to sustain top speed, the sprinter must build up endurance as surely as the distance runner does. Even though it is for only fractions of seconds, the sprinter too must learn to accept pain without letting it stop him. The big advantage that the sprinter has over the distance man is that he does not have to live with pain for long.

The man who runs the 220 or the 200 meters finds that he must build endurance to sustain his speed through a much longer section of his race than the 100-yard dash man. He finds too that he must "live with pain" a little longer. There is still much in that truism that it is the pace that kills, and the pace in the 220 is getting unbelievably fast. We have already seen a record set that is under 20 seconds. As we speed up our 100-yard dash men to get below the 9-second century, we will definitely see such dash men trained to the peak of strength and endurance to bring about the 220 record under 19 seconds. It will come.

FINISHING TACTICS

For decades now, sprinters have been experimenting with various styles of finish at the tape. We have gone all the way from the leap at the tape of a Charlie Paddock to shoulder shrug finish, to forward thrust of the chest with both arms driven backward, to the straight run through at full speed. All of these finishes and their variations, except one, demand split-second timing. The run-through finish is the only one that calls for the athlete to do nothing any different from what he is doing in full stride during the race. In tight finishes, it is possible for such a sprinter to be beaten by a man who is dead even with him in the last stride *if* that other sprinter times the thrust of his chest at the tape exactly right. If the arms

Figure 4a

PAN AMERICAN GAMES, 1967.

Photo by Don Wilkinson, Greeley, Colorado

Track and Field News

Figure 4b

HENRY CARR SPEEDS TO AN EASY VICTORY IN THE 1964 OLYMPIC 200 METERS.

are driven backward, Newton's Third Law assures us that the opposite and equal reaction of the chest will result. Nevertheless, you have only to look at the accompanying photographs (Figures 4a and 4b) to understand what happens when the action is premature. I can see the effectiveness of the thrust finish when it is properly used, but I believe in coaching the run-through style for two important reasons. First, the run-through does not demand any dangerous split-second timing to be effective. Second, the run-through style does not involve *any* deviation from regular sprint form.

Since the 220-yard sprint is now being run around a turn from staggered starts, it has become a different tactical race from the same sprint in a straightaway. One more factor enters into the race, the ability to run on the curve. To assist your sprinter in the race around one turn, you should

Figure 5

RUNNING THE BANKS INDOORS.

instruct him to place his starting blocks as close as he can to the outside line of his lane if he draws one of the inside lanes. This is especially important if the race starts near the turn and finishes in a long straightaway. Starting on the outside edge of his lane will enable the sprinter to run in as nearly a straight line as possible. If the runner draws one of the outside lanes, his angle of approach is not so acute.

You should make your sprinter realize that in the race around the turn he will be placing an unusual strain on his inside leg, not too different from that encountered by a man running the 300 indoors on banked turns (Figure 5). To be sure, the turn outdoors does not throw so much of the body weight over the inside leg as does the banked turn indoors, but the strain is there nevertheless. You should be aware that what is happening is that your sprinter's foot is actually pointing straight ahead, but his weight is being thrown toward the inside of the track. At high speed, the slight turn of ankle against the foot can result in a twisting strain and consequent leg problems, even in occasional pulls. There is a real art to running the turn at full speed. It can be mastered only by actual practice. The sprinter must learn to drive into the turn at top speed while dropping his inside shoulder a trifle and driving his outside arm just slightly across his body. This differs a bit from the straight back and forth drive of the arms you want in straightaway running. Just how much to lean toward the inside and how much to drive the outside arm toward the center of the body must be learned by hard practice in sprinting turns at top speed.

COMING BACK AFTER A MUSCLE PULL

This leads us to another sprint problem that requires very careful motivation from the coach. I refer to that of the sprinter who is returning to action after suffering a pulled muscle. There is quite a bit of misunderstanding among athletes and some coaches as to what happens to the muscle that has been pulled and healed. This depends upon the severity of the pull. If it is a slight one, the muscle itself may not be torn at all. The sprinter may then return to racing in a couple of weeks without ill effects. If the pull is severe, both the sprinter and the coach have a serious problem. Even outstanding medical authorities do not agree on the therapy in such a case. Some insist that the sprinter be kept out of action and treated constantly for three weeks or more. Others advocate having the sprinter jog despite pain for a period of half an hour or more immediately after the pull occurs. This is one point upon which I wish that we could get some definite answers. All that I can tell you is that I have had a hurdler whose leg was black and blue from the rear of the knee to the buttocks continue to hurdle day after day without serious after effects. It was only when I saw the wide expanse of discoloration that I realized that he had pulled. To be sure, I noticed that his hurdling was not up to par, but he definitely was running out a severe pull without even disclosing it. I sometimes wonder whether he would have recovered more rapidly if I had not discovered the injury and made him lay off practice for several days. I have sometimes thought that

I may have slowed down his recovery by making him aware of the seriousness of his injury.

Whatever your belief about proper therapy for the boy with a pulled muscle, one thing you can be sure of is that you have a boy who will need motivation the first time he tries to sprint and perhaps for some time later. You must make the boy realize that the tightness that he feels in his leg is likely to be caused by scar tissue at the point of injury. He must somehow force himself to forget the past injury and his fear of a recurrence. Until and unless he does so, his sprinting is bound to suffer. The boy who has pulled must never be "waiting for another pull." The tenseness that results will be almost certain to bring about the very pull that he fears. Do everything that you can to make him regain confidence.

When a pulled muscle or tendon is involved, you as a coach should realize that there are times when motivation is not enough. No matter how much confidence you inspire in a sprinter, he cannot substitute that confidence for a muscle or tendon that has been severely pulled. You must face the fact that a pulled muscle cannot be repaired. The only thing that can be done for an athlete who suffers a real pull is to help him strengthen the muscles around the one that is pulled. The muscle that has been pulled is like an elastic band that has been broken; it cannot be put together again. If your sprinter says that he heard a sound like a squashed grape and had to stop, you can be sure that he is out of circulation for several weeks. A lesser pull of the hamstring will make him slow down and complain of tightness of the back of the leg. The sore spot is usually at the level of the lower margin of the buttocks. Ruptures at slightly lower levels are in the belly of the muscle and are more serious.

If the pull is slight, a pressure bandage can give the boy a feeling of support and a little more confidence in his ability to sprint. Taping of a severe tear is probably of very little value. Furthermore, the danger of recurrence is great. If of any value the taping must be psychological. There is a great deal of opinion offered by doctors and trainers who specialize in athletic injuries that supports the idea of gradual exercise not more than three days after the pull. Some have insisted that there is therapeutic value in immediate exercise of the leg by a long jog, despite pain, right after the injury. I wish I knew the final answer. I am convinced that the severity of the pull must be considered, but most of the evidence seems to point toward a rejection of immobility in most cases. You have a job of convincing to do in such a case.

I would like to end this chapter on motivation of sprinters by reminding you of one other factor that may help the confidence of your athletes. The sprinter's shoes have always been a source of discussion by coaches.

The number of spikes in each shoe, the placement of those spikes, and the angle at which they are set have all received study. The latest ideas have centered about the advantage of slanting the spikes and making them quite different from those used for many years in the past. The research done in connection with them has indicated that a wedge shaped spike with the wide edge in front and extremely sharp edge in the rear has merit. If you are an experimenter, willing to try for every advantage for your sprinter, you may be interested in investigating the possibility of shoes equipped with such spikes. I think that they are worth consideration.

High motivation in sprinters is illustrated in Figure 6 as Harry Jerome wins the Pan American 100-meter sprint.

Figure 6

JEROME OF CANADA WINS PAN AM GAMES SPRINT.

Photo by Don Wilkinson

| Chapter 2 | # THE SPECIAL CHALLENGE IN DEVELOPING HURDLERS |

WHILE IT IS TRUE THAT THE BUILDING OF THE CONFI-dence of his athletes in any event is one of the major tasks of any coach, the hurdler presents a special problem. If you take a good look at the event as it is run by any good high hurdler, you will quickly recognize the truth in what I say. Not even the high jump with its many styles is as complex an event as the high hurdle race. First of all, we find the hurdler forced to go from his blocks like a sprinter but without the freedom of the sprinter in his attempt to reach full speed. The hurdler cannot, if he hopes to be successful, use whatever stride length he chooses or whatever number of strides he wishes. Furthermore he cannot actually reach full speed before he meets the challenge of the first hurdle. Though his event is vastly differ-ent, the hurdler is somewhat like the weight event men in field events in that he must perform within limits that restrict him. He cannot, like the broad jumper, high jumper, or pole vaulter, take as long a run as he wishes. The first hurdle faces him 15 yards away, and like the field event man confined to his circle the hurdler must achieve what speed he can within that space. But the hurdler differs from the field event man in that he must continue to perform in his event, mustering as much speed as he can within even further restrictions. He then has only three strides to build up speed before he meets his next obstacle, and he must do this nine times in succes-sion before he can sprint unrestricted to the finish line.

Keep in mind also that the hurdler must try to maintain a running form approximating that of the sprinter while clearing a 3′3″ or 3′6″ barrier using a style that is far from that a sprinter uses. If you observe the action of even our best hurdlers above the hurdle you must recognize how unnatural the trailing leg action is in comparison with a straight sprint stride. Leg action above the hurdle, and consequently arm action as well, *must* be different from that of any sprinter. Yet the coach must somehow convince his aspiring hurdler that he must learn to perform this event while losing only approximately two to two-and-a-half seconds in clearing the ten obstacles. He must convince his athlete that he *can* stay close to the hurdle, keep his arms moving in somewhat the fashion of a sprinter's and continue to do this while taking only three steps between hurdles as he goes.

If you as a coach can grasp the complexity and the challenge of this event, you may realize how much of your time with beginners must be spent in convincing them that they too can do what they have seen many other hurdlers do. If you are working with high school athletes who are trying the event for the first time, you are going to have to look for certain signs of promise and then work with each boy with patience combined with unrelenting insistence upon correct form. The main problem you will face will be that of fear, a subtle, discouraging type of fear repeating itself in several ways. You will see it appear in the boy's chopping stride to get into better position to clear the first hurdle. You will see it again in the soaring leap that he takes to clear the hurdle and once more in his flinging of his arms out to the side in fear of losing balance as he lands. You will see it even more obviously when he balks at the first hurdle or runs around the second one. You will see it in his changing to five strides between hurdles when he feels that he cannot possibly get the three-stride coverage he needs. So you will be looking first for an athlete with courage, a stubborn type of courage, one that will enable him to shake off the pain of bruised ankles, then later of bruised knees, and of repeated falls that result in scrapes and cuts of many types. As to other qualifications to be sought, speed and height are obviously of great importance. If you are hoping to produce champions or world class hurdlers, you must consider such things. But above all, even in the athletes naturally endowed with the build and speed that could make them great, you must also seek an accompanying courage and stubbornness that you can build upon to help them achieve their potential.

For years, I have had better than average success in developing high school hurdlers. Rival coaches have always associated Concord Carlisle High School with good hurdlers. Yet I do something with hurdle candidates that might raise many an eyebrow. If this method that I describe next seems too tough an approach for you, I can only repeat that it has worked for me.

It may be motivation of a sort that you will want to try or it may not. At any rate, think about it.

I begin by talking quietly with my hurdle aspirant, telling him some of the things that the event demands. I tell him that he must sprint at the hurdle full speed and then clear it in a diving rather than a jumping action. We American coaches speak of the action as "driving at the hurdle." I like the term that I heard used frequently in Argentina recently. The Argentine coaches speak of "attacking" the hurdle. Because I think of hurdling in terms of aggressiveness and courage, I think that term "attack" carries the implications of what I want to see. I deliberately set a high hurdle at the required distance from the starting line, then tell the boy to get into starting position and clear the hurdle at full speed. I just want to see what he does. I am not worried about his exact form. I am not disturbed if he takes a wild jump at the hurdle, but am very happy if he actually goes over in any form of diving action. I am not too concerned if he takes too many steps as long as they are fast steps. I am unhappy if I see him slow down at the hurdle or balk at it. In other words, I am looking for that display of courage that the boy must have if he is to be developed into a good hurdler. I am hoping to see that courage displayed as he makes a full-speed approach on a legitimate high hurdle. Later in his training I may substitute a hurdle with a padded cross piece or a low hurdle at high hurdle spacing, but not now.

If he cracks his ankle against the hurdle or bruises his knee by hitting the cross piece, I watch closely to see his reaction and even more closely to see him go at the hurdle the next time. I insist that he do it before he forgets the pain of the scraped ankle or bruised knee. Later I may give him some sponge rubber padding for his ankle or a guard for his knee, but *not now*. This introduction to hurdling may seem to some coaches to be mighty rough on a beginning hurdler, but I am seeking something that I can find only under actual racing conditions. There is no easy way to run the high hurdles. It is a demanding, often painful activity. If you must instill courage into your candidate before you spend weeks and months teaching him to hurdle, you had better find this out early. I may not tell the boy who flinches at the hurdle several times in succession that he should forget hurdling, but I know exactly what lies ahead for me in my efforts to make a hurdler out of such a boy. It is not easy.

WORKING TO OVERCOME NOVICE'S FEAR

After you have observed the direct trials given to your hurdle prospect, you know what your job of motivation is to be. If the boy shows fear of the hurdle and persists in jumping it, you must somehow help him to overcome that fear or he will never be a good hurdler. Don't cross him off your list as "chicken" without trying to build up his confidence, especially if he looks like a good bet because of his speed and build. One of the tricks that I use to get such a candidate to overcome his fear is to try moving the hurdle a stride closer to the starting line without letting him know that I am doing it. I never let him run at the hurdle slowly, as some do, because I feel that the hurdles must always be practised at racing speed. There is no relationship between the strides to that first hurdle taken at racing speed and those taken at half speed or even three-quarter speed. The boy must learn to run hurdles at full speed. By moving the hurdle in a bit, I aim to lessen that feeling of being too far away from the hurdle at take-off. Since this stage of the hurdler's development may make or break him as a future point getter, I recommend that the coach be very patient with the boy. If you can get the candidate to take the hurdle in anything resembling a "dive" action while approaching it at full speed, you have made the first big step in building his confidence. After the boy has taken the hurdle without balking, have him keep repeating the action; then ease the hurdle back to its correct distance, again without making him aware of it. If he can still clear it in an acceptable manner at racing speed, start to work on the improvement of his form. If he persists in balking, you have a different problem.

HANDLING THE BOY WHO BALKS

The boy who balks at the hurdle even though you cheat a stride on the distance, and either stops dead or runs around the hurdle, may still be worth the personal attention you must give him. I have found that such candidates can sometimes be helped by setting up a low hurdle at the high hurdle distance and having the boy drive at it in full racing speed. If I can get him to take the low hurdle without flinching, I have him do this over and over again. Then I raise the hurdle to the intermediate height of three feet and have him run at it again. All of my talk with the boy at this stage is to try to convince him that what seems to him to be a long way from the hurdle in take-off is no real problem because of his speed of approach. With both low and intermediate hurdle, I urge him to attack, no matter how far away the hurdle seems to him.

Another bit of motivation I sometimes use here is that of having the boy try consciously for a long stride off the marks. It is disastrous for a hurdler, especially a beginner, to chop his stride as he leaves the blocks. Even experienced hurdlers can run into some trouble by taking too short a first step. I often place a mark on the floor or on the track where the boy's foot strikes as he leaves the starting line. I keep emphasizing the importance of the added few inches in getting the boy into good take-off position. No matter what happens, I will insist upon his running at the hurdle in full speed.

If I can get the candidate to take the hurdle at intermediate height, I may try to bolster his confidence by placing a stick between two hurdles, set opposite each other at the proper distance from the starting line. To encourage the novice, I sometimes cheat a little in his favor in distance when he is about to try this the first time. Because he knows that the light stick at hurdle height will be dislodged easily if he hits it, he may gain confidence enough to attack the hurdle properly. Once he does this, I have him repeat and repeat, trying to convince him that he has licked his problem. Then I put the regular high hurdle into position, usually a foot or two short of regulation distance. I talk to the boy enthusiastically about how easily he has been clearing the stick set at full hurdle height, and I urge him to attack the hurdle exactly the same way. If he clears, no matter how awkwardly he does it, I praise him loudly so that others on the squad may hear and send him back at the hurdle again. I never place the hurdle at its correct distance on this day because I want more than anything else to build the boy's confidence. I carefully avoid doing anything that will upset him and put him right back where he started. Sometimes I will have the boy for whom I still have hopes, run at a single high hurdle set at the shortened distance two or three days before I move it into correct position. I speak of only those aspects of form that will help him to clear the hurdle more easily. Nothing is said about height above the hurdle. I just want to get him over and to make him confident that he can clear. If we are working outdoors, I am careful to have the boy running with the wind at his back, especially if the wind is strong. A strong wind blowing in the beginner's face can be a serious hindrance to him. Don't make the novice's hurdling problems any greater than you have to.

SPEND TIME ON ONE HURDLE

It is my feeling that coaches of beginning hurdlers are often too eager to push the boys into running multiple hurdles. Until the novice has mastered reasonably good form over one hurdle there is little likelihood of his making the three strides to the next hurdle with any success. If the coach tries to rush the beginner too much at this stage, the result may be the undoing of all the careful motivation that has preceded.

FLEXIBILITY EXERCISES AID TWO WAYS

Whether you are coaching a beginner toward acceptable form over his first hurdle or dealing with a star on his way to a championship flexibility, exercises that loosen the hips and assist the athlete to use his trailing leg effectively are of great importance. For the beginner, they are as important as the teaching of the form itself. If this statement seems a little farfetched, you must remember that the novice is attempting a type of action with his trailing leg that is quite different from anything that he has done before. Unless he is unusually supple, he will find this flattening out of the trail leg difficult to master. However, until he does master it, he will have little success in getting down close to the hurdle as he must if he is to get the fast three strides between hurdles. At this stage of his hurdling I insist on plenty of stretching in the hurdle position on the ground, and all other hurdle exercises involving the action of the trailing leg. I also suggest that he spend extra time at home working on the stretch in the hurdling position. The boy should be encouraged to spend a few extra minutes, using his bed rather than the floor as a base for this exercise. You will find that emphasis upon the common hurdle exercises both on the field and at home will aid the boy not only physically but also psychologically. Even the accomplished hurdler cannot do too much of this type of exercise. Suppleness and flexibility are necessities for a good hurdler.

CORRECTING THE HURDLE JUMPER

Besides getting the prospective hurdler started upon a series of flexibility exercises at this time, the coach must devote a great deal of time to getting him to attack the hurdle in the proper manner. To give the beginner the feel of this action, I like to have him stand near a wall and step at it at about hurdle height, bringing his opposite arm into position parallel to the lead leg and dropping his head forward in the manner that he should as he drives at the hurdle in a race. Once he gets the feel of this action, he will learn the difference between attacking the hurdle and jumping it. Some boys grasp this faster than others. Some are still not supple enough to do what they know must be done. If your candidate is very tight in the hips, you can be sure that you have a long way to go before he will ever be a good hurdler. I myself think that this stage of the training is one that may disclose the poor hurdle prospect. Even if the boy shows the necessary courage, his possibilities as a hurdler are mighty limited if he shows extreme tightness around the hips and great difficulty in getting into correct position with the trailing leg.

You might expect that at this point I would have the boy running easily at the hurdle and concentrating upon correct form above it. But no, this is not my system. I can see some value in a coach's shortening the boy's approach run and having him concentrate on correct hurdle clearance, but for several reasons I prefer to continue to insist on full speed approaches. Oh, I may at first substitute the padded hurdle or the hurdle with the loose cross piece at this stage of the training, but I seldom allow any slowing down of approach speed. It is my conviction that the timing involved in the hurdling action is so different at a slow pace from what it is at racing speed that the boy gets a false conception of the rapidity with which drive from the take-off foot, lift of the lead leg, positioning of the trailing leg, and all arm action must be completed if he slows down his approach. I will often show the beginner loops or movies of good hurdlers to help him to grasp the form he needs. I may take Polaroid camera shots of the boy himself to show him how he looks as he tries to clear the hurdle. I am convinced that the boy must have a clear picture in his own mind of just what he should be doing in his drive at and clearance of the hurdle. Again you may think that I am mighty rough on a beginning hurdler. Perhaps I am, but I know that I have made many a respectable looking hurdler in a couple of weeks using just the tactics and motivation that I have described here.

BUILDING CONFIDENCE FOR THE THREE STEPS

When I am satisfied that the boy is clearing the first hurdle in acceptable form, driving over it with good forward lean and fairly good arm action, I tell him that he is now ready for that part of the event that will determine whether he is ever to be a good hurdler. I talk to him enthusiastically about how much he has improved in his form at the first hurdle and I emphasize how this improvement should make the three steps between hurdles much easier to handle. I try to make him aware of the rhythm of the three strides by having him listen to the sound of a good hurdler's steps between the barriers. I believe that this is a very important point in the motivation of the beginner. He must become conscious of the rhythm of the three strides and think in terms of them before he falls into the troublesome five-step pattern. What is in the boy's mind is mighty important.

If the coach can help the athlete establish the rhythm of the three steps in his mind, the first efforts of the novice are sometimes highly improved.

The boy with the rhythm firmly in his mind will be trying to take only three steps even though he finds it difficult. I have found it helpful at times to stand near the hurdle lane and either clap my hands loudly in the desired three-step rhythm or simply shout, "ONE! TWO! THREE!" as the boy comes off the first hurdle and heads toward the second.

Occasionally you will find a boy who is tall enough and supple enough to take the three steps with very little effort, but usually the teaching of this stage requires a great deal of patience. Although it is true that the distance between hurdles can be covered very easily in the required three steps, the coach will find it difficult to convince some beginners that it can be done. There are, however, several things that you can do to bring the boy through this key stage of his hurdling. It is here that careful and persistent practice over the one hurdle should pay off. If the boy has been driving correctly at the first hurdle, check to see whether he is landing on his heel. If he is, you will notice that he stops for a fraction of a second upon hitting the ground. This forces him to gather himself for the three-stride sprint after having lost valuable speed as he hits. Correct this by insisting that the boy keep his head well forward and that he does not lift it while above the hurdle. Preventing the block that results when he lands with his weight behind his lead foot is extremely important. It is important in the form of even a very good hurdler, but it is doubly important to the boy who is struggling to master the three-step pattern (Figures 7a and 7b).

Figure 7a

JOHN ALDEN OF CONCORD-CARLISLE HIGH SCHOOL, MASSACHUSETTS.

Figure 7b

JOHN DUNCAN OF CONCORD ATTACKS THE HURDLE.

When you have worked with your novice on coming off the first hurdle with his body weight kept forward so that he will land on the ball of his foot, you will find that he will have much more confidence in his ability to negotiate the distance in the three steps. Because the landing is so often a problem for beginners, I have made a practice of supplying them with plastic heel protectors. These will prevent heel bruises and avert the added problem of the athlete's trying to get drive from an injured foot.

The next factor that contributes greatly to the athlete's success in getting the three-step pattern is what happens to his trailing leg *after* it has cleared the hurdle cross piece. If the athlete has cleared the hurdle in reasonably good balance, and landed on the ball of his lead foot correctly, you will notice that his weight settles for an instant on the whole foot, but pay special attention to what he does with *the knee of his trailing leg*. You will help him to achieve the three fast strides between hurdles much sooner by hammering at the fact that the knee of his trailing leg must be lifted very high as he lands to permit that long first stride toward the next hurdle. Unless you can get him to get that knee very high, almost shoulder high, he will fall into the error of the short first stride. For a beginning hurdler, this is disastrous. If you study the good hurdlers closely, you will notice

51

that they have two long strides followed by a slightly shorter one as they gather for the clearance of the next hurdle. The confidence of your beginner will be helped immeasurably if you can get him to do three things well. They are: (1) attack the hurdle at full speed, (2) come off the hurdle in good balance so that he lands on the ball of his foot and is being driven forward, not backward or upward, and (3) get very high knee lift of his trailing leg so that he can get a long first stride after landing. (See Figure 8.)

Photo by Don Wilkinson

Figure 8

RELAXED ATTACK. DAVENPORT, U.S.A.—PAN AM GAMES, 1967.

You will find that many small faults remain to be corrected as you proceed with your beginning hurdler. These may include his arm action above the hurdle, his tendency to clear the hurdle too high, his inclination to turn his body too much toward the side of his trailing leg when he is above the hurdle, and also a difficulty caused by this same turn of the body, a landing with his foot pointed toward the side rather than directly ahead. You will also be bothered frequently by the boy's tendency to gallop instead of sprint between the hurdles. Don't confuse the novice by trying to point out too many weaknesses at once. Work on the key points and take up the lesser ones as the boy improves.

Perhaps you have now reached the point with your beginner where he is getting over the first hurdle in fairly good style and also getting his three steps between the two hurdles quite well. It has been my feeling that there is one more stage of learning and confidence-building needed and often neglected by coaches. The boy has now mastered clearing the first hurdle correctly and his three-stride approach to the second hurdle, but he is doing this with the help of a full 15-yard sprint approach which gives him momentum to clear the first hurdle and retain enough speed to help him build speed for the second hurdle. But don't forget the problem presented by the third hurdle and all others that follow. The boy must now clear a third hurdle with only the speed he can generate in three strides. You will find that quite often a boy who can get his three strides to the second hurdle will balk at the third one or others along the way. You must again help your beginner by emphasizing the added need of correct form in the attack on the second hurdle and the high knee lift of the trailing leg from good balance and forward drive over the lead foot. This phase should not be neglected. Even if you do not have an indoor track program, you can do much for your beginning hurdler by having him work frequently over three hurdles in the gym.

HANDLING THE PROBLEM OF WIND CONDITIONS

It is surprising how often you will hear track athletes complaining about climatic conditions for practice or competition. The same boy who will slog through mud in pouring rain in a football game will often be the one moaning loudest about the cold or the rain or the wind during track season. Strangely enough, the chief subject of complaint is likely to be the wind. Perhaps the emphasis placed upon the wind as a factor in the acceptance or rejection of records in several events in track and field may have something to do with the athlete's consciousness of the effects of wind upon his performance. Sprinters constantly complain about having to sprint against the wind. Some even go so far as to blame track architects for setting up the sprint areas so that "the wind is almost always in the athlete's face." Yet it is the high hurdler who has perhaps the most legitimate cause for alarm when he must run into a strong head wind. When his speed is cut down, when his stride is shortened by inches, he can be in far more serious trouble than the sprinter.

First of all, we must remember that the hurdler has only 15 yards in which to build up speed to the first hurdle. Indeed, he has even less than 15 yards for his take-off point for the first hurdle cuts that distance by more than two yards. Tests have shown that the sprinter usually reaches top speed at about 60 yards from the starting line. The high hurdler has only about 13 yards before he must attack an obstacle. He then has three strides to build up enough speed to attack another obstacle and so on over the full flight of hurdles. The wind plays no favorites. If it is in the sprinter's face cutting down his speed, it is almost certain to be doing the same to the hurdler. The hurdler, especially if he is relatively short and needs full stride length to get into take-off position in the eight strides that he has, finds the wind more of a problem than the sprinter. The loss of a few inches in each stride means to the hurdler that he may be a foot or more short of his regular take-off mark at the first hurdle. Each hurdle that follows must then be affected. The margin of loss builds up and the hurdler finds himself not only losing distance badly needed but also losing the speed that might enable him to gain back the lost space. Even very good hurdlers will turn in poor performances under such conditions. Think then about what this must mean to the neophyte. He is having troubles enough making the necessary 8-3-3- stride pattern under normal conditions; he is often seriously upset by practicing against the wind.

Because I recognize the need of confidence the beginning hurdler has, I do everything I can to make his job easier. Whenever possible I will have the beginner running the hurdles with the wind at his back. Thus the inches are added to his strides, and making the first hurdle in eight and the remaining hurdles in three strides not only seems a little easier but actually *is* a little easier. When he has gained the necessary confidence to run the correct hurdle stride pattern, then I will let him face the challenge of practicing with the wind against him.

OVER-DISTANCE HURDLING

In many of the high school meets today, the high hurdler is faced with the necessity of running trials and finals and sometimes even trials, semifinals, and finals. Certainly under such meet conditions, the endurance of the athlete is highly important. But some coaches lose sight of the fact that the single hurdle race itself is a demand upon endurance as well as speed. I believe that the coach must plan work for all of his hurdlers to build up their endurance. I like to include in such work not only regular sprint interval training for all of my high hurdlers but also what I might call "hurdle intervals." Quite often I set up five or six high hurdles on the yard lines of the football field, placing the first one on the fifteen-yard line or putting it on the five-yard line and starting from the back line of the end zone. The others are then placed the usual ten yards apart on the correct yard lines. After setting up five hurdles in this manner, I reverse the procedure and set up another five in the proper spacing heading back toward the end zone. The hurdler can then run his five hurdles in one direction, move into position for the return five hurdles and with only the break it takes to get into starting position, continue to run sets of five in interval fashion. It is also possible to vary this by having the athlete run a couple of flights of five and then jog the distance beside the hurdles before starting another series. Several sets of hurdles can be used to permit your hurdlers to work on these intervals on the football field without tying up the track on your sprinters or distance men.

Besides using the hurdle intervals described above, I have also worked on building endurance in my hurdlers by setting up eleven hurdles instead of ten, giving them the extra hurdle as well as the extra running distance to cover. I have found this latter practice to be helpful in motivating the athlete who tends to fade after the seventh hurdle. I should caution the coach using these hurdle intervals and the over-distance hurdling to avoid overdoing it because the hurdler will tire rather quickly and when tired can take some nasty spills. You should perhaps begin with about three or four flights of five with a short rest and then a repeat. As the boy gets stronger, you can give him more repeats and even add a sixth hurdle to each flight to make the intervals a little tougher. Having the boy run on the grass covered football field will lessen the chances of injury if the boy tires and starts to hit hurdles. You can add a little extra motivation to the practice by setting up the hurdles in this shuttle fashion and having two or three hurdlers working together for a bit of competition. You can have a watch on the hurdler as he does these intervals or forget the watch, as you wish. The value of these shuttle hurdle intervals as preparation for the running of the infrequent shuttle hurdle relay is obvious.

WORKING THE LOW HURDLER

Because of the concerted move on to drop the low hurdle race from high school meets, there does not seem much to be gained by spending time here on the motivation of low hurdlers. At its best, the race is more a sprint than a hurdle race. Hurdle form is not really involved in the way that we use it in the high hurdles. You can be sure that unless you have a candidate with very good sprint speed you will not have much success with him in the low hurdle race. The race does resemble the high hurdle race in that the boy must usually cover the distance to the first hurdle in ten strides. Some very tall boys can reach the first hurdle in nine strides, but beware of forcing even the tall boy to try it in nine if he has to overstride to do it. It might be enlightening to you to time the boy using nine strides to the first hurdle and then again as he takes ten. The seven stride pattern between hurdles seems to be the best by far.

As you prepare your low hurdler, you should keep in mind what I have said about high hurdle practicing at full speed. I can see no real value in running low hurdles at less than full speed. Only bad habits can result from letting your hurdler revert to nine strides between hurdles as he runs them in three-quarter speed. It seems far more sensible to me to have him run repeats of half the low hurdle distance over fewer hurdles but at racing speed than to let the boy change his stride pattern by working at half speed or three-quarter speed.

With low hurdlers as well as high, work on the grass covered football field can be beneficial. To get the regularity of stride that the low hurdler needs, he can use the yardage lines on the football field with or without the hurdles set up. Just as we often have long jumpers practicing over low hurdles to get regularity in their run to the take-off board, so too it makes sense to have the low hurdlers do some work on the long jump runway. Consistent stride length at racing speed is what the low hurdler needs; any type of practice that will help him gain confidence in his ability to sustain the stride pattern through the race distance will be good motivation.

As for low hurdle form, the nearer the boy can come to making his clearance of each low hurdle merely an extra long, high step, the better he will be (Figure 8a). Of great importance in his retention of speed is his coming off each hurdle in good balance. The hurdle height is of no such significance as it is to the high hurdler. Furthermore the low hurdler has added yardage in which to build up speed to the first hurdle as well as more yardage between hurdles in which to regain that speed between hurdles. Speed, regularity of stride, and good balance are of greatest importance in low hurdling, but do not overlook the need of endurance training for this event. Since the low hurdles are usually run at 180 yards in high school, it is obvious that any meets that call for trials, semi-finals, and finals can involve endurance. Shuttle hurdle intervals on the football field and plenty of the type of interval sprint work given to the 220-yard man should be planned for your low hurdler. Some of his sprint interval practice can be given to him by means of endless relay practices with your sprint relay team, of which he may well be a valuable member.

RUNNING THE INTERMEDIATE HURDLES

Few high schools in the United States have yet gone to the use of the intermediate 400-meter or 440-yard hurdle race, but this race or a shortened version of it may soon be with us in high school track meets. The old idea

Figure 8a

LOW HURDLERS IN ACTION.

that this is too demanding a race for high school boys seems to be dying out with the prejudices against the high school two-mile run. It is obvious that the high school runner in proper condition can handle the intermediate hurdle race as well as any other.

Though the intermediate hurdle race does not place such a premium on good hurdling form as the high hurdle race, it does pay off good hurdling as the runner tires. Getting the athlete well prepared for this race demands plenty of emphasis upon the type of workouts given to the 440-yard runner. This race is a tiring combination of speed, respectable hurdling, and endurance. The form more closely resembles that used in the low hurdles than that used in the highs, but some attention to good use of the trailing leg and good forward lean as the hurdle is attacked will pay off.

In working on the striding of your intermediate hurdler from the starting line to the first hurdle, you should be aware that more variation is common in this than in any of the other hurdle races. From 21 to 24 strides may be observed, depending on the build of the hurdler. You will want to time your athlete as he uses various stride patterns to determine which gives him the best time and the best balance. Above all be careful not to let him overstride. The race is tiring enough without paying the price for overstriding.

Though it is possible for a very tall intermediate hurdler to cover the distance between hurdles in 13 strides, it may be wiser to have him take 15. Most of our best intermediate hurdlers now take 15. Someone may come along, blessed with the combination of great height and great speed, and with 13-step hurdling smash all of the existing marks for the race, but he will be another of the supermen who upset all our thinking. Dave Hemery combined 13-stride and 15-stride hurdling in his Olympic win. The high school intermediate hurdler should almost certainly be working on 15 strides between hurdles. I believe that good motivation for the high school boy in this event would be to spend about 75 percent of his time on speed work and endurance and 25 percent of his time on hurdle practice (Figure 8b).

Figure 8b

DAVE HEMERY (CENTER) COMBINING 13 STRIDE AND 15 STRIDE PLAN FOR NEW WORLD'S RECORD 48.1 IN 400 M. INTERMEDIATE HURDLES IN 1968 OLYMPICS.

Photo by Don Wilkinson

KEYING ON THE HEAD POSITION

In all hurdling, but especially in high hurdling, good form is revealed by the position of the athlete's head as he approaches, clears, and lands. The observant coach can aid his hurdler very greatly in high hurdling by keying on the athlete's head position. It is interesting for the coach to place a cardboard just below his eyes to blot out everything except the hurdler's head as he sprints toward the hurdle, clears it, and sprints for the succeeding hurdles. It is soon obvious that the good hurdlers will show no sudden rise of the head as they clear the hurdles. You will find it not too easy to determine just when the good man was over the hurdle. The dip of his body as he attacks the hurdle will keep his head on almost the same plane as when he was sprinting.

You will also find that by watching only the hurdler's head as he runs you will be able to notice any backward motion of the head as the boy lands on his lead foot off the hurdle. The momentary jolt that results if he lands on his heel is quite evident in the motion of the boy's head. It is easy to observe any turning of the body toward the trailing leg side as the boy's head will turn slightly too. I suggest that in your efforts to help your hurdler you spend a little time watching only his head. There is much of value to be learned from such observation.

	COACHING
Chapter	AND STIMULATING
3	MIDDLE DISTANCE AND
	DISTANCE RUNNERS

WHEN WE SPEAK OF MIDDLE DISTANCE AND DISTANCE running these days we have to do it almost with tongue in cheek. There is no event left in the ordinary track meet that is not becoming a sprinter's race, *relatively speaking*. The 440-yard run which was once considered a middle distance race is now being run by a man sprinting the first 220 in about 22 seconds and then finishing in less than 23 seconds for the second half. The half mile has now become a combination of two 53-second quarter miles. Even the mile run is now demanding four sub-sixty-second quarters. The two-mile run is reaching the stage where a world class athlete must put together two 4:15 miles to be reasonably certain to win. High school quarter milers are breaking 47 seconds; high school half-milers are hammering at 1:50 for the distance, and several high school milers have broken the once unbelievable four-minute barrier. Two-mile runners of high school age are already under 9 minutes. The coach today may well ask himself whether there are really any *distance* races left. He may be looking at his average squad manned by average runners and saying, "Maybe I should take my fastest sprinter and make a miler of him. That's the only pace he can handle."

MOTIVATING THE BEGINNER

There can be no denying that races at all distances today demand speed. But the coach should not make the mistake of thinking that the boys who can run a 10.5 for the 100 yards can automatically become the 48-second quarter milers or the 1:55 half milers. It is not true that whoever runs the 55-second quarter will have no trouble putting together four 65-second quarters to run a 4:20 mile. There is more than pure speed involved in any event from the 300-yard run indoors to the two-mile run outdoors. Every one of the races from the 440 through the two-mile run is a race demanding *sustained* speed. The temperament of the athlete becomes a decisive consideration. Sprinters are notoriously fretful about running over distance, even in practice. To such boys the thought of running a half mile or a mile is frightening. Perhaps we coaches are to blame for letting our sprinters develop this fear of distance. Perhaps the day is coming when we will have to try convincing them that they are actually better suited to becoming half milers than 220 men or that they show more promise of carrying the mile pace than they do of handling the 440. Perhaps, but I am not ready to concede this yet. I am convinced that there is such a thing as a talent for distance running even as we know that there is God-given talent for sprinting. This seems to me to be more than a mere problem of motivation. I can not bring myself to believe that we can find another Peter Snell simply by taking a 21-second 220 man and making him into a half miler. I definitely don't think that a coach can take any 52-second quarter miler and make him into another Jim Ryun. These young men are not average in any sense of the word and 50-second quarter milers are run-of-the-mill. The Snells, the Lindgrens, the Liquoris, and the Ryuns are above average in every sense of the word. In talent, in dedication, in motivation, they stand above the crowd. We coaches can no more make our average runners into such super-stars than we can expect just any basketball player to become another Bob Cousy or Bill Russell, or any high school baseball player to become another Sandy Koufax or Willie Mays. We coaches may lift a runner above expectations, but only a special few will be the stars. It is a phantasy to think that every high school track team is filled with boys who can become world class athletes. World class athletes are rarer than that. The intriguing thought is, however, that maybe this squad that faces me, the coach, may have one hidden right now. That's what makes coaching so interesting.

MOTIVATION AND RACING TACTICS FOR THE QUARTER MILER

Judging from the speed at which quarter miles are now being run, many coaches are thinking of the 440 as a race very little different from the 220. In other words, the race has become a sustained sprint, according to such coaches. They therefore plan work for their quarter milers concentrated around speed workouts. With so much speed now demanded in top flight competition in the 440, there would seem to be merit in gearing the athlete both mentally and physically for sprint type racing. Certainly speed work must be a substantial part of the preparation of today's and tomorrow's quarter milers. But as I ponder about the great emphasis on speed training for quarter milers, I am bothered by the realization that endurance has to be a factor in any race of this distance. Some coaches will argue immediately, "But the race now involves *sustained speed;* there is no longer any recognition of the 'coast' or 'float' as a part of the 440." I agree that coaches are now trying to convince their runners that they must run the opening 220 of their race as close to maximum speed as they can and still not fold in the home stretch. They are trying to make their 440 men run all out for the whole distance.

DEVELOPING MEDIOCRE TALENT

Two things bother me about such attempted motivation. They arise from my thinking very deeply about what is indicated by the careful research done by Franklin M. Henry in his study of sprinters and sprinting. He found first of all that men generally reached their top speed about six seconds after leaving the starting blocks. He found also from his research that it is physiologically impossible for the runner, after reaching top speed to maintain it for more than 15 or 20 yards. I know that Henry was studying sprinters and no doubt considering races in which the athlete was attempting to reach full speed *as soon as possible* and to sustain full speed *as long as possible.* In the 100-yard dash, so little endurance is involved that such running is a "must." In the 220, there may be a little more doubt about where to attain top speed and try to sustain it to the finish.

If you think a moment about the two points shown in Henry's research, you should realize that the second point he made is of great importance to the quarter miler. If the runner after reaching top speed can sustain it for only about 20 yards, where in the 440 do you want him to try to reach top speed? Does he ever really reach top speed in the 440 or does he strive only to approach "the breaking point" and therefore enable himself to carry the pace that he has set over a much longer distance? Should the quarter miler train like the dash man to get to top speed as soon as possible in the race, hold that top speed for the longest time possible, and then finish the distance with as little loss of speed as he can? Would it be better for a 440 man to make an effort to reach *top* speed at about the 220 mark, sustain it for the 15 or 20 yards and *then* finish with as little loss of speed as possible?

Should he instead forget the idea of the race's having two 220 sections to it and think of it as not being divided into halves at all? Perhaps we should be forgetting the long prevalent idea of a first 220 to be run at one speed and a last 220 to be run at another. Since the race is obviously not a pure sprint race, would we not be better off as coaches to think of the race as a unit? I have always been interested in the fact that so many quarter milers, especially in high school track, will look mighty good until they reach about the 300-yard point of the quarter mile and then fall apart. I am sure you can recall many a college runner doing the same. Maybe we should now forget the old ideas about two 220 sections of the race and start thinking about the value of preparing our quarter milers for a gradual build-up to top speed around the 300-yard area and a sustaining of that speed as long as possible, and *then* a drive to the finish with as little loss of speed as possible.

If we think of the 440 in this way, we will soon see the necessity of training our quarter milers so that they can sustain their top speed as long as possible as well as conditioning them to lose the least possible speed in that final hundred yards or so to the finish. To help your quarter miler reach his potential following such a plan of running, you will have to know rather accurately what his top speed is. You will have to work within the possible limits of improvement of his speed by helping him to start a little better and to gain the tenths of seconds afforded by the correction of running faults. In other words, you will need to handle him during this phase of his training just as you would one of your sprinters.

STIMULATING THE STAR

The next stage of his training might involve a change of thinking by both you and the athlete. Henry mentions in his study the possibility of a man's continuing at top speed for about 15 or 20 yards before he starts to lose it. Here is an important area for consideration. We coaches may do well to concentrate upon this phase of the man's running as a possible area for improvement. Not every runner, be he sprinter or quarter miler, can sustain top speed for a full 20 yards. Some show a slackening of speed in ten yards, others in about 15 yards, and only superbly conditioned athletes in about 20 yards. Yet think of what this means in terms of advantage to the runner who can retain top speed for 20 yards against one who starts to lose it after ten. For better use of our athlete's top speed, we may be wise to work on this phase of his running regardless of the distance of his race. What we are talking about, remember, is the utilization of the best running of which he is capable.

THE DANGERS OF STRESS

Don't deceive yourself into thinking that this improvement will come easily. There is more involved here than merely urging the runner to make an effort to run a few steps farther at full speed. What I have said in Chapter One about getting sprinters to run at their *real* top speed is a part of the problem; getting them to sustain that top speed after they reach it calls for the athlete's confidence in his ability and the coach's close study of his runner's action. It means also the careful combination of flexibility exercises and strength building to prepare the runner physically for what he is trying to do. Furthermore, for the quarter miler, it means the insistence upon a training program to build up his endurance as well as his speed.

RACING TACTICS IN THE 440-YARD RUN

Recent efforts by top flight quarter milers point definitely to some changes in racing tactics in the 440. Against ordinary competition, the good quarter miler can still run easily just off the outside shoulders of the leaders and then when ready take command of the race and leave them far behind. There are still some fairly good quarter milers who will coast through an easy first 220 of the race and then come with a rush from far back to win in crowd-pleasing fashion. But before the coach joins in the back-slapping crowd that gathers around the finish line to greet such an athlete, he had better realize that all such a quarter miler proved was that he could have stayed right with the pace all the way and won much more easily. The only reason that he succeeded in his showy finish was that he was far better than his opponents in the race regardless of racing tactics. Like an outfielder in baseball who loafs under an easy fly ball and then has to race to make a spectacular grab at the last moment, the 440 man who falls far off the early pace is just making his own job tougher.

The question is often raised of how far a lead at a given pace would be impossible for the athlete to make up, regardless of his spectacular sprint. If you think back very far you will realize that there are many more of these "blazing finishers" who just miss catching the leader than there are those who win the race. Some time ago I wondered what mathematical possibilities were involved in such racing tactics. I talked the matter over with a fine mathematician in my own school system and I learned some interesting facts.

SPECIAL CONSIDERATIONS

Let's assume that one boy runs the first 220 yards of his race at a pace of 8 yards per second and continues at the same pace through the 440. You might think that the boy who eases through the first 220 of his race at 6 yards per second and then lets go for a 10-yard per second pace in the last half of the race would end in a tie with the first boy at the tape. Such a conclusion would be erroneous.

The first boy runs his first 220 in about 27.5 and holds that pace all the way for a 55-second quarter mile. The second boy, who might seem to be able to offset that steady pace with the tactics described above, would be at a surprising disadvantage. It can be proved mathematically that the second boy after loafing that badly in the first half of the race would have to finish the race with a 22-second 220 to approximate 58 seconds for the quarter. Actually if he were to run his first 220 so foolishly, he would then have to run his last 220 in better than world record time to catch the 55-second man.

Of course, it is highly unlikely that a quarter miler with the speed necessary for a 22-second finishing 220 would ever trot through a ridiculous 36-second opening 220, but this extreme case will show what a burden the man faces by falling too far off the pace. What has been given here as an extreme case applies just as surely to a more normal type of race. Let's suppose that the quarter miler from Team A is a boy who likes to break out front and take over the pace with a fairly good opening 220. He runs the first 220 in 24.5 and then falls off to a 27.5 to finish the quarter in 52 seconds. The Team B runner is the boy who likes to hang back in the first 220 and come with a rush from there. If he ran his first 220 in 27.5, we might think that he could catch the Team A boy by finishing with a 24.5. We must realize, however, that the Team B runner has allowed his opponent to open up a three-second gap and has given that runner a lead of 20 yards or more. He then has no alternative except to run that last 220 in 24.5 if he wants to catch his opponent at the tape. Any delay even in the first ten yards of that second 220, will mean failure for him. Let the Team A man run better than 27.5 for his second furlong and 24.5 will not be good enough to catch him. Actually, if the team B man delays his acceleration *even a single second* he will be unable to win the race without bettering 24.5 while his opponent goes over 27.5 for the remaining distance.

Suppose we look at this matter of pace and position from another angle. In many high school meets, and in some college meets as well, it is not uncommon to see a 50-second quarter miler allow a rival who has also run a quarter in the same time to build up a long early lead. The first boy has several things working for him. He has managed to get himself clear of the pack if the race is not run in staggered lanes. This means that he can run without obstruction at the pace he has planned. His chief rival, on the other hand, now has more than the problem of correct acceleration to bother him. If he has stayed with the pack, he may well find several others ready to move at the same time he wants to. If he encounters any jostling at all, it may impede him and his task of overtaking the leader becomes even more difficult. Now unless he goes below 23 seconds for his final 220 he is in real trouble. Let the leader merely hold to a 26-second final furlong after a 24-second opening one and he will be the winner. With this in mind, the coach should remember that there are not too many high school quarter milers able to come up with a 23-second 220 around a turn. As the quality of the runners improves, the more urgent it is to heed the dangers of permitting too long a lead. If the quarter milers involved are capable of running under 50 seconds, the trailing man is faced with an almost impossible task if he allows his talented rival more than a second's lead at the half way point in the race. Should he start his rush any later in the race, only the collapse of the leader will enable him to win the race.

MOTIVATING AND PLANNING TACTICS FOR HALF MILERS

We now approach the races that are more dependent upon endurance than upon speed alone. If we think of the 880 as a race run in about 1:47 and 1:48 in top flight competition and in most high school races in not better than 1:54 or 1:55, we can see that we are dealing with two 440's averaging in fine college competition about 53.5 or 54 seconds and in fine high school competition about 57 or 57.5. Taken separately, such quarters do not demand phenomenal speed. Thousands of high school boys have the speed to run a 53.5 quarter, but it is a different matter to run one and then to have the stamina to add another one to it. Even the half mile then, admittedly being run faster and faster, still makes its greatest demand upon the runner's endurance.

Perhaps you will not agree fully with me that races from the half mile up to the two-mile run demand great emphasis upon the building of endurance and far less emphasis on speed work. I realize that there are different approaches to distance running. On the one hand we have Lydiard who turned out great middle distance and distance runners, using no weight training, no calesthenic exercises of any consequence, and putting the emphasis on endurance. As you may know, he even had his middle distance men doing marathon training. On the other hand, there is Igloi who has also developed great middle distance and distance runners but by a system based largely on comparatively short repetitions run in large numbers at very fast paces. Certainly the fact that both coaches have succeeded while using quite different types of emphasis leaves the average coach somewhat confused. Both the total mileage emphasis found in Lydiard's training system and the speed repetitions stressed by Igloi will develop endurance. The big question with the United States high school or college coach is likely to be, "But which method works best?" The answer seems to be that much depends upon who is doing the coaching. It is very important that you as a coach decide on a system of training that seems to you to best meet the needs that you and your athletes have. It is very difficult to sell your runners on a training program that you yourself doubt. My feeling is that you should set some goals for your middle distance runners, consider the time that is available for practice, and set up a program in which you have faith. Forget the idea that there is something magic in the training schedule of Peter Snell, or Jim Ryun, or Ron Clarke. These are exceptional men, dedicated, *determined* to be world class runners. In all of your coaching career you may never have anyone to approach them. Your task is to do the very best you can for the athletes that you do have. I personally agree with those coaches who insist that the training schedule must be geared to the individual. I cannot accept the idea that the adoption of any given training schedule whether it be Ryun's, Kuts', Snell's, or Joe Unknown's will insure dramatic success with the runners on your squad. To motivate your middle distance runners, you must offer them training schedules that are fundamentally right for the improvement of endurance, for the increase of speed within the possible limits, and for the practice time available.

We read often about the stress that middle distance and distance runners must overcome through workouts. Perhaps we should also consider realistically the stress under which United States high school and college coaches must work to develop such runners. My own feeling is that the very nature of our track program here is an obstacle in the way of our greater success with our middle distance and distance men. The demands of our track schedules with their frequent dual meets (sometimes two a week) and their week-end relay carnivals, invitation meets, league championships and class and state championships put any coach into a dilemma. Our immediate goals force us to choose between bringing our athletes along as fast as possible to meet the challenge of our rivals or pointing them toward more distant goals advantageous to the athletes themselves. I am convinced that most of us are rushing our middle distance and distance runners along too fast. I am convinced that the development of the kind of endurance needed for world class competition must be through a long-range program. I would like to see the athlete given more time to get his body accustomed to the stresses that he must meet in top flight competition. Even though the great runners can take the rigors of a training program such as Snell's or Elliot's or Ryun's, the average runner cannot and when he tries to do so, he becomes discouraged very quickly and decides that such training is not for him.

Even the coach who is concerned with bringing his ordinary middle distance runners along successfully may need to revise his thinking a bit about their basic background. Many coaches in this country are considering the 880 so much a speed event now that they are neglecting the build-up of the boy that should precede the speed work. A few weeks of cross-country running in the fall and a light program of overdistance work often provide all of the background the half miler gets before he is rushed into speed work. Fortunately, the speed intervals, as Igloi has shown, do aid in the building of endurance, but it would be well for the average coach to realize that Igloi frequently puts his runners through two workouts a day and as a result the total amount of work his athletes get is quite substantial.

Thinking of the psychological effects on the average half mile candidate in high school, I fear that a work program geared too heavily on high speed repetitions would prove too monotonous and as a result mentally tiring. It is true that quite a few of our high school and college runners are adopting the double workout. Some are willing to do the early morning work and follow this with a regular workout in the afternoon. But the number is not great in most schools. Furthermore the demands of studies are often so great that the boys frequently find that they are unable to devote that much time to running. World class competition in the 880 does without a doubt demand more and more of the athlete's time for practice, but the more ordinary runner will not usually accept the double workout program so readily. And that leaves us just where, you may ask.

My belief is that the coach must think in terms of a program that sets a goal two or three years away. He should try to encourage the boy to build gradually toward a peak, setting certain interim goals for the athlete to reach. The boy should be kept informed about the plan and not suddenly rushed into a speed-up to meet competition in a certain coming meet. In other words, the coach cannot have both ends; he cannot set up a long-range program and drive his athlete into short-range preparation too. The confusion of goals forced upon the high school coach in the United States by the demands of his schedule is a real problem. I think I am in agreement with some very fine coaches when I say that the 880 and the mile run and all other distance runs should be approached through long term programs of development during which the runners are first given a base of miles and miles of work and then sharpened for specific races. It might be interesting to see the reactions of some of our most famous trainers of race horses if you were to suggest to them that they enter their horses in two or sometimes three races a week while still trying to get them ready for such a race as the Kentucky Derby. But is not that just what we are doing with many of our track athletes? If the trainer of horses would shudder at the thought of piling race after race on his four-legged stars, should not we coaches begin to be more sensible about the demands we make upon boys?

To set up a training program for half milers in such a way that it will have motivational value, the coach should consider carefully the various individuals with whom he is working as well as the nature of training needed for success. Since the half mile run definitely comes within the area of racing that involves oxygen debt, it will be worth while to understand just what effects good training can have on this factor. The coach should realize that training *does not* bring about extension of the limits of oxygen debt. It does aid economy of movement so that the need of oxygen is less. A well-trained athlete can meet a reduced oxygen expenditure with higher oxygen intake, thus going more slowly into oxygen debt. The trained athlete will reach his oxygen debt limit later than an untrained athlete, but he cannot extend that limit. The coach should have clear in his own mind what is being accomplished by the training and make his middle distance men aware of what is happening to them. I would not advise the coach's going into any long scientific explanation to the athletes, but he should be accurate in what he does explain to them. He should know that a runner can postpone the oxidation of lactic acid until it builds up to an amount requiring about 15 liters of oxygen. When we speak of oxygen debt, this is what we mean.

As the concentration of acid increases, the athlete feels increasing discomfort until finally the muscles do not respond. This is the fatigue that the middle distance and distance runners experience, whereas the 100 yard-dash man runs entirely on oxygen debt. He has usually very little or no oxygen intake. Most sprinters actually hold their breath during the whole race. Middle distance and distance runners *depend* upon oxygen intake.

We know that the normal top breathing capacity of the lungs is about 4 liters per minute, but we must also realize that great athletes are not normal. They can often take in more oxygen than the normal man. Dr.

Thomas Cureton in his study of over two hundred champions found that they could not force themselves into any greater oxygen debt than could ordinary college students. With this clear in his mind, the coach should be aware of what he is trying to accomplish through training. He should realize that highest endurance can be obtained by training the body to adapt to gradual stress. This calls for long and patient training, continued regularly and persistently. Through good training the body becomes better able to tolerate respiratory distress. This is where will power comes in and should explain Zatopek's gruelling practice to make himself rise above this distress.

Too often coaches are looking for miracles. They set up training programs for their middle distance and distance men and abandon them too quickly because they learn that some other coach is having success with some other system. The result is that the runners become confused and the coach's own program never gets a real chance. Don't make the mistake of upsetting your runners. Set up a program that you believe in and stick to it until you have ample evidence of its weakness. Don't change with every new idea that comes along. If a system seems effective, notice what aspects of it may be incorporated in your own system to make that more effective.

As you plan your workouts for your half milers, keep in mind that middle distance runs differ from distance runs only in that they demand carrying speed over varying distances. The 880-yard run actually involves faster quarter miles than the four-minute mile. To carry the pace demanded in good half mile running, I feel that the work planned should include plenty of background in cross-country and *fartlek* before the boy is put into a tough schedule of interval training. You should consider the condition of your individual athlete and base your work program on that, keeping in mind the goals you hope to reach at certain points along the way. I believe that it is a mistake to subject the runner to too many times trials at full effort. If you believe in pointing the boy toward certain big races, set your sights far enough in advance to bring him to a peak for them.

RACING TACTICS IN THE 880

When runners get beyond the 440, the margin of lead they can allow their opponents is greater than in the quarter mile. But that margin is not as great as might be supposed. As has been pointed out earlier in this chapter, the runner who is doing ten yards per second is doing the 100 in ten seconds. True he is in motion and not slowed down by the mechanics of starting, but he must still have quite a supply of natural speed to carry such a pace for any appreciable distance. It may come as a bit of a shock to realize that any runner carrying a steady pace of eight yards per second will finish the half mile in 1:50. Obviously then, any runner who hopes to challenge a boy of such capability will find himself in trouble if he allows the leader as much as a two-second margin during the early stages of the race. What this means in terms of pace is that he would be giving up about 17 yards and even with no other adverse factors such as jostling opponents, delay in acceleration of his own pace or the like, he will have to run a 53-second last quarter to catch the leader. Actually he would have to better 53 seconds to win the race. It is also important to understand that the 53-second pace would have to be maintained without interference or such tactical errors as running too wide or cutting around opponents between him and the leader. For most high school runners, a quarter that fast in the 880 is mighty rough.

Among the most common errors made by inexperienced runners who have fallen dangerously off the pace in the opening half of a race is that of trying to close the gap in one sudden burst of speed. Instead of accelerating gradually through a large portion of the race, they panic and make an all-out bid that drains them of their reserve. Then when the leader makes his move at the end of the race, they have nothing left with which to meet it.

It is extremely important to a middle distance runner to know how long his opponent can sustain his fast pace and still have something left for a final drive at the tape. Though some coaches dislike the idea of planning a race, I am not one of them. I think it is very helpful to a half miler or any other runner to know just where his chief opponent likes to start his final bid. He can then upset his rival's planning by jumping him just before the point at which he likes to make this bid. This can be very disconcerting to a runner who is thus forced to start his final kick before he wants to. Such a move obviously must come from your boy when he has stayed close to the pace, not when he has first made a burst from far back to get into striking position.

Many coaches love to have their man strike from behind. They know the psychological value of having their runner just off the outside shoulder of the leader. This position has a great deal of tactical merit. To a certain degree the runner in this striking position keeps the leader guessing. The trailing runner knows just when he plans to strike, but the leader is never sure. The trailer is in position to meet any bid that the leader wants to make. In such a race, the trailer is not likely to set any meet record unless the leader has gone out at a stiff pace and held it throughout. This is a tactical sort of race and not one aimed at record-breaking time.

If your runner has kept with the pace and held himself in good striking position at the outside shoulder of the leader, he has another tactical advantage. He is forcing any other runners who have designs on the win to go into the third lane to get around him. Your boy does have to be alert to any sudden burst of speed from a runner behind him, but he can meet it by moving in his own lane and thus forcing the bidder to run wide. It would be a tactical mistake, of course, to run directly behind the leader because any boy coming up on his outside would have your boy in a natural box. He then would have to be the one to go to the outside to get at both the ones in front.

Though it is true that unexpected moves by an opponent can upset strategy in a planned race, I still like such a race. The middle distance runner who is thinking about his planned moves and the strategy of position is less likely to be thinking about his own aches and pains. I like things that help to divert the distance runner's thoughts from his own discomfort. Don't overlook the psychological value of planning a race with your middle distance runner.

WORKING WITH DISTANCE RUNNERS

Not long ago, I read a very interesting article in which Jim Ryun expressed his ideas about the oft-emphasized need of conquering pain in distance running. Some other great distance runners have been quite dramatic in describing the mounting distress and pain that the sub-four minute mile brings. Ryun commented emphatically, "Too much is made of the pain stuff. Running doesn't hurt that much. I've tried to explain to people that there is more satisfaction than pain in a hard workout, but I guess too many of them can't understand that work can be satisfying." He went on to remark that if running hurt as much as people seem to think it does, he would not have gone out for track in the first place.

When Ron Clarke came back to the United States for his return match with young Gerry Lindgren, he looked up Gerry to interview him in connection with his own book *The Lonely Breed*. When Clarke returned to his room some time later he was heard to remark about the training program that Lindgren described to him, "That fellow is either a physical marvel or the greatest con artist in history."

Lindgren had been telling Clarke about his four-week "crash" schedule of three workouts a day. Coach Tracy Walters had convinced Gerry that to have any chance against the Russians he must be willing to work all out. The program that Lindgren detailed to Clarke totalled about 250 miles a week. Even Clarke, who is no slouch himself when it comes to hard workouts, gasped when he heard what Lindgren was doing.

I am sure that many of you coaches who read such accounts of training schedules such as Lindgren described, or who think of the look of agony upon the face of the great Emil Zatopek as he drove himself to his victories in the Olympics, will find Jim Ryun's remarks about the overemphasis on pain in distance training rather hard to take (Figure 9). As you think of

Figure 9

EMIL ZATOPEK—TWENTY-ONE TIMES WORLD CHAMPION, THREE TIMES CHAMPION OF EUROPE, AND INNUMERABLE TIMES CZECHOSLOVAK NATIONAL RECORD HOLDER.

your own distance runners, you may swallow hard and wonder just how to suggest a workout such as those handled by Lindgren or Ryun and at the same time tell them that pain is not involved. It would be well to consider carefully Jim Ryun's comment that it is not that pain is not involved but rather that pain has been made "not important."

I had a chance to talk with Zatopek himself at the American-European track meet at Expo 67 in Montreal and as I saw him smiling and amiable, I thought back to all of the accounts of his punishing work schedule during the years of his greatness and back also to his own description of his determination to conquer pain and to force his body to do what he demanded of it. There are the accounts of his deliberately holding his breath for exceptionally long periods of time to accustom himself to the distress. I thought of his pounding away at repetitions of 200 meters and 400 meters in astonishing numbers and the comments current at that time that the man was killing himself. But as he stood there before me in his light blue suit, he looked far from dead. He looked as though he could even yet prepare himself to run with the best in the world. I thought too of his remarks that "Pain was not important. Man must master his body."

It would be foolish to think of Zatopek, Snell, Lindgren, and Ryun as ordinary men. These are the great ones, the gifted ones, the dedicated ones. They are not to be found in every school or in every state, or indeed in every country in a given year. But with me there is always the nagging thought that there are many more like them scattered throughout the world waiting for the right coach to come along to give them that starting push toward greatness. What can we coaches learn from them that can be used to motivate the mediocre?

It seems to me that we must begin by stressing more the type of philosophy of pain that Jim Ryun expresses. We must talk our average distance men into the recognition that the body can respond to stress gradually and that, given time and training, it can reach the point where it is capable of workouts that at first seemed impossible. But I do not subscribe to the idea that we should hand a training program of Ryun or Lindgren or Zatopek to any young high school distance prospect and tell him to start work on it. I say this even in relation to any young prospect, enthusiastic and dedicated though he may be. The training schedule he uses is not the key to a Ryun or a Lindgren, nor will it be the secret of success for your distance runner. This sort of thinking seems to me to be in reverse. This idea that all a coach has to do is to get hold of the training schedule of one of the great ones to find the solution of his problems is very common but also very foolish.

How then do we go about motivating our own runners, keeping in mind that after all there is only one Olympic champion per event even though there may be literally thousands of runners all over the world dreaming of being that one. Certainly the dream must come before the fact, but the dream must be founded upon fact too. Those runners that you and I have may have to face the fact that even a state championship may be a distant dream for them. Anything higher set as a goal would be self deception. We coaches must motivate toward achievement, not toward self deception. The budding distance runner on your squad must be moved toward a goal that he can hope to achieve. He must be started on a training program that is geared to his capacity. He must be able to see progress.

To be successful in motivating the ordinary distance running candidate, the coach must first win that athlete's respect. He can do this only by treating him as an individual and setting up a training program that is reasonable for that individual. This means certainly that the coach must study his prospect with some care and with some intelligence. It seems to me that one of the biggest mistakes we coaches make is that of dropping too easily into a training pattern that groups runners of all calibres and of various stages of conditioning. There are times when some runners benefit by running with a group, all of whom are doing the same type of workout. There are times also when the runner will make progress by being grouped with runners who are not all doing the same workout. But there are more times when the athlete must feel that he is getting consideration as a person, not just a part of a mass effort.

First let's give some thought to what values there may be in having the new distance prospect work with a group. If you have several candidates just beginning work and all in relatively the same physical condition, you can bring them through the early stages of their training by giving them group workouts that will extend them just a little as they begin to learn what demands distance training makes upon the body. This stage, during which the athlete suffers the pains and aches of the first weeks of training, will be more bearable to him if he sees others alongside him who are having the same troubles. The old cliché that misery loves company is not so bad in this training situation. If the coach can kid along with this starting group to make them forget their aching muscles and straining lungs, he will have brought them past the first barrier to distance running. This is the point at which the new candidate is reluctant to agree with men like Ryun and Zatopek that pain is not important. Unless the runner is an unusually self disciplined young fellow he is going to find the sore muscles and fatigue a mighty personal thing. He still has to learn to control his body. This is a stage of training during which the coach, if he is in reasonably good condition himself, can at times run along with his group of neophytes to help them through this early training problem. For many years I made a practice of running with the beginners in both cross country and other distance running to help ease them through this first challenge. And believe me, *it is a challenge*. This is the time when the athlete is not ready to suffer alone. He will make more progress in a group of runners like himself than he will alone. Though this might be thought of as group or team training rather than individual training, it involves really the development of the individual runner through the association with coach and group. The coach, while running with the group, can aid the individual runners even more effectively by shuttling back and forth among the runners, encouraging them individually and checking closely upon the condition of each one. There is a fine opportunity for motivation presented in this type of workout.

After the first two or three weeks of conditioning in the type of group work described above, it is time to begin the workouts geared to the needs of each candidate. Sooner or later the distance runner must face the fact that it is *his* body that must be controlled and mastered. What other men do may help him psychologically to be a little better able to master his weaknesses, but in the final analysis, he must battle alone (Figure 10).

Figure 10

ARTHUR DULONG OF HOLY CROSS COLLEGE.

Photo by Blue Ribbon Sports

Since the athlete's mastery of himself is a personal problem, he should at this time be given an individual workout schedule. I believe that this is the time to start the distance runner on a second phase of his training, that of taking him away from the group and making him meet the stress of training alone. Here again, the coach needs to realize that the athlete is undergoing a new phase of stress. If he has studied his athlete well during the first stages of his training, the coach will have formed some decisions about the type of work to give him. It should be enough to help him to progress but not enough to discourage him. Remember, it's really pace, not distance, that is the greatest drain upon the body. This stage of training should be the one during which the runner is given cross country running, *fartlek* work, and not too strenuous interval training. It seems to me that at this point, the coach is wise to avoid mention of the total distances covered in workouts. He should keep the athlete thinking in terms of the short periods of fast running involved in the cross country work and *fartlek,* not about the six or eight or ten miles covered as a total. He should keep the boy's mind on 220 intervals or 440 intervals rather than upon the total mileage he is covering in all.

There is one important consideration here in the interval training that the coach should not ignore. That is that the recovery time between intervals is of great importance. If the athlete is to progress and help his body accustom itself to the stress, he must allow himself only enough recovery time to be ready for the next interval. There are various ideas of how this can best be handled. Dr. Woldemar Gerschler of Germany has conducted long and exhaustive studies of the effects of running and rest upon the development of the runner. From this study he has come up with a theory known as the Gerschler-Reindel Law. His tests indicated that in the course of physical exercise, the heart beat reaches 180 per minute as a limit during physical exercise. The athlete then was permitted one minute and thirty seconds to return to 120 or 125 beats per minute. If a longer time was required for recovery to this stage, Dr. Gerschler contended that the effort demanded was either too violent or too long for the athlete. Dr. Gerschler stressed the importance of some physical activity during the recovery period, as this is the factor that strengthens the heart. He suggested walking as a good activity in the early stages of training, followed later on by slow jogging.

I found it interesting however, to talk with Dr. Warren Guild, President of the American Society of Sports Medicine, about this belief of Dr. Gerschler's. Dr. Guild claims that by actual testing with his own son, Nat, he found that instruments which he placed on his son showed heart beat well above the 180-beat limit mentioned by Dr. Gerschler. Furthermore he added that at such times, his son, far from showing ill effects, would suggest that they pick up the pace. He does concur with Dr. Gerschler in stating that the recovery phase of the training is what is most important.

For a long time, it was believed that athletes who had very low pulse counts were fine distance running prospects, but later tests revealed that many top distance runners had pulse rates well above the 38 or 40 per minute once thought so significant. It has been shown that training will result in lower pulse rates. My own belief is that this low pulse rate may be valuable in checking the athlete's physical condition at the time rather than his value as a distance running prospect. I find it very hard to discount the low pulse rate as unimportant because I found that almost every very good distance runner that I coached in high school showed much lower than average pulse rate, usually in the 40 to 50 beat range and some even lower. It seems to me that there is room for further study of this point.

Dr. Gerschler is convinced that the check of the heart beat and the recovery time permitted should be exact, and he has gone very deeply into the matter in his training of athletes. Others have been unwilling to set up so strict a check upon the athlete's condition. Dr. Gerschler in a talk with P. Sprecher which was written up for Fred Wilt's fine book, *Run Run Run,* stated that he considered the Swedish training method of *fartlek* not exact. Nevertheless, when used efficiently, *fartlek* has been the basis of training for many fine distance runners. The same is true of other well known training methods such as Lydiard's, Igloi's and Bowerman's. It is exactly this obvious success with widely different methods of training that has convinced me that future training schedules for distance runners will become highly individual plans, perhaps best described by Ken Dougherty as "Holism" in training.

To you as a coach this means that you will be considering the physiological testing of the athlete like Dr. Gerschler, the natural inclinations of the runner as found in *fartlek,* the flexibility of day by day scheduling seen in Igloi's plan, the basic background "marathon training" used by Lydiard, and the psychological factors emphasized by Dougherty. If this thought sounds intricate and demanding upon the coach, it is only because the times demanded of future distance runners will continue to improve and force the more complete dedication of both athlete and coach. High school runners breaking four minutes in the mile and under nine minutes in the two mile are living evidence of the intense training ahead for those who will follow and undoubtedly surpass them. What is important to us as coaches of athletes below world class calibre is that the demands upon our coaching knowledge and the efficiency of the training methods we use with our more ordinary distance runners will gradually become more critical. If we are not blessed with the great ones, we will be forced by the improvement of competitive standards to make our training methods more efficient.

I am wondering at this point whether the thought may be running through your mind that coaching in the future may well be so challenging as to be almost frightening. The great demands upon the track coach's time which will come if more and more individual planning and help must be given to the many athletes on the squad is quite a prospect in itself. How then is any coach going to meet such demands while still doing his usual high school or college teaching?

I talked with Bob Timmons, now known throughout the world of track as the coach of Jim Ryun, not so much about the training schedule of Ryun but about the training schedule he uses with the less talented distance runners on his squad. He told me of a method he uses, which, though it may be thought of as a group workout, seems to me to be very valuable as motivation of the individual. I consider it very valuable to any coach who is wondering how in the world he can treat his distance runners as individuals in a group situation. Coach Timmons has set goals for the individuals in their interval training and has urged each of them to think in terms of improving the average time for the interval in the workout. Thus a boy may be running quarters at, let us say, 70 seconds but with the purpose in mind of turning in quarters averaging 69.5. Jim Ryun may be running on the same track but working on a series of faster intervals. The runner though working on the same track with Ryun and in a group relatively like himself will still be carrying out an individual plan. He is not being discouraged by trying to handle a Ryun-scale workout; he is not alone in his workout, but is grouped with others of his own ability yet working toward a previously set goal. This seems to me to combine the group workout with highly motivated individual effort. I am sure that it brings about real progress, especially progress that the athlete can see himself. Used with discretion, the plan can be made to work by any coach, but it is no more the final answer to distance running training problems than any other system. Unless the coach has evaluated his individual runners carefully and worked out realistic goals for them to aim at, he will have only limited success with this plan. Used incorrectly, it can become little more than a new type of day-by-day time trial. As an innovation, it may capture the interest of your squad and some of the individuals on it, but overused, the plan can become as much a drain upon the athlete as competition every day would be. (See Figure 11.)

Consider the plan for what it really is, a method of giving purpose to the individual's part in a group workout. Unless you are caught in a

Figure 11

JIM RYUN AND TEAMMATE USING THE INTERVAL CLOCK.

situation in which you must institute a crash program to develop distance
runners, make your candidates understand that their goals should be set
some time in advance. The runner's ability to lower his average in the
interval sets by half a second on a given day should not be considered an
indication that he is now ready to work on the next lower goal. Weather
conditions, mental condition of the athlete and other factors should all be
evaluated before the next step is taken. I would be in favor of having the
boy continue on the same level for several days before I considered his
goal reached. It would be unwise to expect progress in every workout. The
boy should be made to realize this fact also. His progress should be seen
as something to be achieved gradually, not something to be made in a
grand rush that puts too much stress upon his body. Remember that mental fatigue can be relieved through hard exercise but real physical fatigue
can not.

The coach who is checking pulse rate should realize that this rate for
a given exercise at a given pace will be higher in hot surroundings than in
cold because the flow of blood to the skin to expedite heat dissipation will
be greater. In evaluating the averages run by his distance runners who are

using Coach Timmons' method, the coach should understand that climatic conditions can have quite an effect upon the workout. Many are inclined to forget that a series of 440's run in almost ideal conditions is quite different from a series run in cold blustery weather on a rain-swept track. It would be foolish to expect the results under the latter conditions that one might get under the former. Some might think this too obvious to need mentioning here, but I have seen too many coaches disturbed over what they considered a poor workout, never taking into consideration the weather conditions at the time. A little common sense is needed in this relationship. On the other hand, the coach should not be too ready to baby his runners and lead them into thinking that only under certain weather conditions can they perform effectively.

Whatever the system the coach adopts, he will understand better what he is accomplishing with his athletes if he studies carefully the findings of Dr. Hans Selye on stress and its effects upon the human body. He will then better understand that endurance results from progressive training and is not due to inheritance. He will realize that highest endurance can be obtained by training the body to adapt to *gradual* stress, since it is through such training that the body becomes better able to tolerate pain and respiratory distress. He will then see why the training of the athlete should be holistic because will power is related to endurance and therefore should be specifically trained. He may understand better that overtraining may occur after more than 12 weeks of hard, progressive work. Dr. Thomas Cureton has been quite specific in his insistence that the amount of work done be long enough and hard enough to increase oxygen transport to the muscles. The coach who really wants to understand what he is doing to his athletes should study seriously what has been written by Dr. Selye and Dr. Cureton. He will then begin to appreciate the fact that man has just begun to test the limits of the human mind and body. When we realize that the energy in one gram of matter equals the normal annual output of energy of 14,000 human beings, we really have something to conjecture with. What if man eventually learns to use the energy stored within himself? Would we have any conception of what our world records might be? Far out as this may seem, have you ever thought of the possibility that man may have latent energy stored within himself not too unlike that in coal, or oil, or the atom. Perhaps the athletic feats of future man will be tied in with his use of human matter. If you think this too fantastic, have you considered that man is constantly being forced to discover new limits of his capabilities and then, in the case of some human beings, to transcend them?

If at this time you think that I am about to submit to you a series of workout schedules for your distance runners, aimed at the achievements they must reach in the future, you are wrong. I repeat, this is an individual matter. *You* must determine what your athlete needs and plan his schedule accordingly. If you study your candidate well you will learn something about the stresses that he faces in his daily life and you will realize that the athlete striving to win is *adding* stress to that which disturbs him already. Dr. Selye has pointed out that no one can escape stress. All forms have some impact, but the impact can be good or harmful. The effects of it, not the stress itself, constitute the danger.

It is interesting to find that Dr. Selye states that during the alarm stage the body's hormones produce chemical compounds keying you up for action and then causing depression. He says that both may be of practical value to your body. Thus it is important to the athlete to be "keyed up." If you have ever laughed at the coach's "pep talk," perhaps this may force you to think again. If nervousness does reach the athlete and aid in keying him up, but not too high, it can thus help him toward a better performance.

Much has been said and written about oxygen debt and its effects on distance runners. Putting it very simply, a runner can postpone the oxidation of lactic acid until it builds up to an amount requiring about 15 liters of oxygen. This is what is known as oxygen debt. An increasing concentration of the acid causes increasing discomfort until finally the muscles do not respond. This is fatigue. Runners in the 100-yard dash run entirely on oxygen debt. Most of them actually hold their breath during the entire race because it is easier to run with the chest held high and the abdomen tight. Tests led to the disclosure that man cannot exhaust himself before about 50 seconds or about a quarter mile. At shorter distances the runner is not limited by his supply of energy, but by how fast he can use it. As the distance of the race increases, the oxygen debt becomes less important. Distance runners depend largely upon oxygen intake. It is known that the normal top breathing capacity of the lungs is about four liters per minute. In this connection, you as a coach should remember that the great athletes are not normal. They are exceptional. Such men can often take in 16 percent more oxygen than the normal person. Dr. Thomas Cureton in testing more than 200 champions found that Roger Bannister had the highest intake rate of all those tested, yet he was also the weakest of them. Dr. Cureton found that the 200 champions could not force themselves into any greater oxygen debt than could ordinary college students. Thus it can be seen that training results not in extension of the oxygen debt but in economy of movement which makes the need of oxygen less. Trained athletes can therefore meet a reduced oxygen expenditure with a higher oxygen intake than the untrained man. This means that they go more slowly into oxygen debt and reach their limit later. The coach then should avoid any misconceptions about raising the limits of the oxygen debt in his runners and realize that what he is doing is making the movements more efficient while helping the athlete to increase his oxygen intake.

Much study has been given to the effects of high altitude upon distance runners. Medical staffs from many countries of the world made careful studies of the problem as their athletes prepared for the 1968 Olympics in Mexico City. Put into language that we coaches can understand, what happens is that when men climb to high altitudes, the gases within the body tend to expand as pressure drops. The intestinal gases force the diaphragm upward which hinders breathing. For this reason, there was concern expressed by athletes of all low-lying countries and demands for provision for practice at high elevation to ready the distance runners for the demanding races in Mexico City and other places of similar elevation. Some encouragement has been gained from the fact that in the Peruvian Andes there are Indians who work steadily at half the normal ration of air. It would be impossible for the unacclimatized person to duplicate such efforts. Studies have shown, however, that a period of gradual training under high altitude conditions can aid the distance runner to meet such racing conditions. It has also been learned that after training and racing in such high altitudes, the athlete is likely to improve his times when he returns to lower levels.

Though you as a coach may think that such facts are of no concern to you, you should not miss their relationship to your own problems with distance runners. The runner breathing the rarefied air is not too different from your distance runner as he approaches oxygen debt limit with limited oxygen intake. He is not too different from your miler running indoors in smoke-filled arenas, nor from distance runners in the North practising and racing in severely cold weather. If you are faced with having to prepare your distance man for a trip to some race to be run under very different climatic conditions than your own, you may wish to prepare him by simulating the conditions under which he is to run. To prepare for the intense heat of Rome during the 1960 Olympics, Thompson of Great Britain spent long periods in a heated bathroom as part of his training for the 50-kilometer walk. American girl swimmers practised in pools with temperatures and humidity raised to simulate the conditions under which they expected to race.

If you feel no need of preparing for such extreme conditions, then at least consider the extremes in climate as they affect your distance runners' regular training and vary your demands upon them.

Before going into the discussion of racing tactics for milers and two milers, I would like to sum up for you the key points of any work schedule that you should offer your distance runners. I know of no really outstanding track coach who is not insistent that the work begin with cross country in the fall of the year. Whether you have your boys compete in the sport or simply plan the fall cross country work as part of the year's schedule is up to you.

More and more coaches are getting their distance men accustomed to workouts twice a day. If possible, the double workout daily can pay dividends. I am not too enthusiastic about a program requiring three workouts a day even though the time might be available for them. I doubt that you will find many like Lindgren willing to take such a punishing schedule.

Fartlek type work certainly has some value if emphasis is placed on the correct factors. It is not an aimless workout but one which should require the athlete to engage in several different types of running, including hill work, short, fast spurts, sustained running at moderate speeds, and easy jogging for recovery.

Though some coaches do not encourage weight training for distance runners, I think that it can be used to develop the upper body of the distance runner, especially the arms and shoulders. Men run with their arms as well as their legs. As racing season approaches, the coach should have his distance runners ease up on the weight training.

My conviction is that distance runners should be pointed toward a few big races each season and not expected to be in peak condition all season long. If race horses cannot be kept at a peak for more than a few selected races, it seems unreasonable to expect boys or men to do more.

In the course of your interval training program, I believe that days of great stress must be followed by days of recovery running. It will be helpful to your runners if you can locate a variety of training areas, using certain ones for certain purposes. It is my feeling that as the racing season approaches the coach should put the emphasis upon shorter recovery periods between intervals rather than upon great numbers of repetitions. Faster intervals should be demanded later in the season.

In attempting to help his distance runner make the best use of his energy, the coach should emphasize relaxation during the training itself. He should be trying to help the athlete eliminate excessive body sway and faulty arm action. He may be wise to overlook individual eccentricities such as those shown by Bruce Kidd of Canada, Ron Delaney of Ireland, and Emil Zatopek of Czechoslovakia. If you have ever seen these runners you will remember the flopping arms of Kidd, the peculiar little trotting style of Delaney, and the facial expressions of Zatopek. I cannot recall noticing that the mannerisms of these runners did any great harm to their running.

Finally, make every effort to build up the runner's faith in himself by letting him see his progress. Give him immediate goals that he can reach quickly but also eventual goals that must be approached slowly and patiently. If you can lead your distance runner in this way he will have faith in you as well as in himself.

RACING TACTICS FOR DISTANCE RUNNERS

Like the half miler and the quarter miler, your miler and two miler must always keep contact with the leaders. He should, if possible, know his opposition, and be aware of the point in the race at which his most threatening opponents like to make their real bid for the race. He should be taught to keep himself in such a position in the race that he can make his own move just when he wants to make it. Nothing can be more frustrating to a runner than to be ready to move, only to find that he has been caught in a natural box and cannot get out of it. I feel that more attention should be given to this point than coaches usually give to it. Far too many distance men lose races because they are unable to make their drive when they want to (Figure 12).

By the same token, an experienced distance runner can often force an inexperienced runner to stay to the outside of the track and thus cover more distance than he should. If the coach will keep in mind the distances between staggered starts given to runners in the 440, he will have a clearer idea of just how much extra distance the miler covers if a smart man on the pole makes him run for very long in the second lane. I am sure that you have seen many milers race the pole man through the whole back stretch, staying wide all the way.

Some coaches dislike setting up a racing plan for their miler or two miler. They feel that any unexpected tactics used by the runner's opponents can disrupt that plan and force a complete change. There is a certain amount of truth in this contention, but I like to discuss some form of racing strategy with my distance men. I hope to accomplish certain specific things by such planning. First, I believe that concentration upon a racing plan helps to take the man's mind off his own feelings. He becomes intent upon making certain moves at certain times and is given a little added confidence by the thought that he has a measure of control over the race. If he is thinking about the plan he may well be less tense than he would other-

Figure 12

SUAREZ OF ARGENTINA PASSING MOWATT OF JAMAICA
IN THE 10,000 METER—PAN AM GAMES.

wise be. Second, the man with planned racing strategy can take the initiative in the race. If he moves suddenly and with authority, he can shake up the opponents. I am also aware that his opponents may upset the plan by making certain unexpected moves of their own. But if the coach has done a good job of motivation, he will have made it clear to his runner that he must not expect to have everything his own way. He must be prepared for some effort by his opponents to prevent his controlling the race. He must be reminded that a move by an opponent may force him to make his own move five or ten yards before he expected to. This should not disconcert him because he may have actually brought about this move before his opponents wanted to make it.

WHEN THE LEAD IS VALUABLE IN DISTANCE RACING

It has always been surprising to me that so many distance runners are so reluctant to take the lead in a race. Many of them feel that by leading they leave themselves wide open to the trailing runners in a race. My contention is that they would not feel this way if they took the lead with the right purpose. First of all, any runner who is trying for a record is making a mistake if he runs a tactical race in which much jockeying for position is involved. If the runner knows that he is superior to the rest of the field, he must take the lead if the others are deliberately slowing the pace. In fact, he *must* take the lead early in the race. If he falls back into an early slow pace, he will have to come up with a spectacular performance in the final stages of the race. Any runner who sincerely wants to attack a record must be aware of an early slow pace and move out to take command. In other words, the prospective record breaker *must* take the lead to set the pace he needs.

On the other hand, a runner should take the lead if he wants to set a slow pace. If he gets out in front, he may be able to shape the race to his own pattern. Unless the other runners are aware of his strategy, he may be able to run the first couple of quarters at a pace that will help him to conserve his energy for the final 220 yards and the strategic use of the superior speed that he knows he has.

Too many distance runners overlook the importance of meeting any challenge that comes in the final 220 yards of the race. To me this is a cardinal sin. I hammer incessantly at the point that no distance runner can reject a challenge in the final furlong of a race. This is no time to think in terms of pouring it on in the final hundred yards. Any runner who takes the lead at this stage in the race has confidence that he can hold his pace to the finish line. I consider it the biggest tactical mistake in track to let him take control without a challenge.

MOTIVATION AND
Chapter TACTICS IN
4 RELAY RACING

ANY COACH WHO IS REALLY INTERESTED IN DEVELOPING
a good relay team should realize that this is a rather complex situation.
He is faced with the necessity of motivating and preparing four individuals
to fit into a small team. Surprisingly enough, four outstanding sprinters do
not immediately assure the coach of a fine sprint relay team. Though other
types of relays call for the coach's understanding and shrewd placement of
his runners, the sprint relay is more demanding upon his knowledge of his
men than the others. There is too little margin for error in the sprint relays
to allow for misplaced personnel. Whether the coach is trying to hide his
weak man on an average relay team or mold four great speedsters into a
fine sprint team, he must consider the types of men he is dealing with.

INDIVIDUAL AND TEAM EFFORT INVOLVED

Actually, the coach has more possibilities in the juggling of his runners than he might think. He might want to stick to the traditional relay
order, putting his fastest man at anchor and his second fastest at lead-off.
Even then he must decide whether to run his weakest man second or third.
His decision might well be based upon the nature of that weak man. If he
knows that the man is a front runner, he may like the idea of running him
second, in the hope that his fast lead-off man will hand him the baton with
a lead that he can hold on to. On the other hand, the coach may feel that

he would rather put the weak man *third,* giving two better runners a chance to build up a more substantial lead for the weak man. He would then have his fastest man at anchor, ready to hold the lead if the weak man has dissipated most of it or to battle back if he has lost the margin supplied by the first two runners. Still another possibility here is that of running the weak man last when he is one who likes to run in front. If the team's best sprinter is exceptionally good, he may upset the opposition by running the third leg and building up a big lead for the weak man. In sprint relays like the 440 or the 880, especially the former, the lead given to a weak man may be enough to bring him home ahead. The obvious danger in such tactics is that your weak man may well be running against the strongest men on opposing teams.

WORKING FOR COORDINATION

Some coaches like to shuffle the order in other ways. They will sometimes lead off with their strongest sprinter in the hope of getting away in front of the pack, thus putting the stress on the other teams who must cut down the lead. There are many possibilities of switching runners in the relays, but moves should be made on the basis of the coach's understanding of his runners.

Some sprinters will almost unconsciously ease up if they find themselves in front by a comfortable margin. When relays are run in staggered lanes as most sprint relays now are, this can be very dangerous. The runner by virtue of the stagger may think that he is well in front, only to discover when he hits the stretch that he is running practically even with his opponents. The coach must work on men who make this mistake, insisting upon their going at top speed all the way. One way to motivate such a sprinter to a better performance is to put your weak man next in the running order. Your front runner can then be motivated toward top performance by reminding him that his teammate must have a good lead if he is to keep the team in contention. Too many coaches lose sight of the real importance of the lead-off man. The anchor spot is considered of first importance, yet the truth is that the toughest assignment is that of the lead-off man. He must run his leg without benefit of a running start and he is likely to be running the longest distance if he delivers the baton to his teammate past the middle of the passing zone.

Though coaches often spend plenty of time on starts with their sprinters, they sometimes overlook the wisdom of having these same sprinters practice starts while holding the baton. Even the holding of the light baton in the hand on the starting line will bother some starting sprinters. It is for this very reason that I have often had all of my sprinters, even alternates, doing quite a bit of starting with the baton. Beginners are often uncertain about how to hold the baton at the starting line. Coaches who spend plenty of time on perfecting baton passing should not neglect practice in starting with a baton (Figure 13).

Another important consideration the coach faces in relation to his lead-off man is that of where to have him deliver the baton to his teammate. If his first man is very good and his second man only fair, he may wish to take full advantage of his lead-off man's superior speed and have him carry the baton as far as possible. If he plans to have the pass completed as near as possible to the far end of the passing zone, he will be giving the weak man as short a running distance as possible, especially if he should have him deliver the baton to the third runner in the back section of the zone. If the weakest runner is the second leg runner, the coach can give him help on both ends of his leg in this manner. Though this would seem to be sound strategy, it is not without its weakness. The coach must also remember that the lead-off man, if he carries the baton the extra yards, is a tiring runner about to pass the baton to a fresh one. Some thought must be given to whether anything is really gained by such a plan. I believe that it has good motivational value. The coach can point out to the weak man that he can race his hardest since he has the shortest distance to carry. He can point out to him also that he has the advantage of a longer space within the passing zone to get up speed while he awaits the pass. He can also be shown that he will have less ground to cover when he is tiring at the end of his leg, because he will be passing to his teammate in the back end of the zone.

THE USE OF THE ALTERNATE

The rule which now permits the relay man to use the additional space outside the passing zone to get up speed before taking the baton is an important advantage, but it is one that requires much work and careful timing to be really valuable. Many relay teams are finding to their sorrow that it is very easy to complete the pass too soon and be disqualified as a result. Others are learning that if the outgoing runner starts too soon he may be out of the passing zone before his teammate can deliver the baton. Some, especially in high school relays, are finding that after reaching top speed they are forced to slow down to avoid going out of the passing zone before the exchange is made. There can be no doubt that the coach must spend plenty of time working with his relay team, *including his alternates,* to perfect this all-important phase.

Courtesy of Martin S. Dworkin and Scholastic Coach

Figure 13

THE RELAY START.

If you have watched any of the big relay carnivals held in the spring in various parts of the country, you must have noticed the surprising number of types of passes used by competing teams. Even in the sprint relay you will observe that several kinds of "blind" passes are employed. Not only are there differences in exchanges in which some incoming runners bring the baton *up* into the hand of a receiver who has his hand and fingers extended downward while others coming in bring the baton down into the outstretched hand of a teammate who holds his hand palm upward, but there are also variations of these two common exchanges. Some holding the palm up will turn it to the outside slightly; others will point the hand straight back. Some using the palm down will have the incoming runner sweep the baton upward and into the hand between the thumb and the fingers. A few teams can still be found using the hand-on-hip reception with the incoming runner slapping the baton into the pocket formed by the receiver's hand with the finger tips just touching the hip (Figure 14). You will also see wide use of the "inside" pass in which the outgoing runner will take the pass from his teammate's right hand with his own left (Figure 15a and 15b). Some teams on special occasions will stick with the conventional left to right pass. Still other teams will alternate right to left and left to right passes in the same race.

91

Figure 14

THE "BLIND" PASS—JOHN ALDEN AND JOHN DUNCAN
OF CONCORD-CARLISLE HIGH SCHOOL.

Figure 15a

MARTY MILNER OF HOLY CROSS CARRYING THE BATON.

Figure 15b

MILNER PASSES TO TEAMMATE USING INSIDE PASS.

You will hear a variety of reasons offered by coaches for their use of the passes they employ. Frequently you will find the term "free space" being used. What is meant by this is that coaches are concerned with getting maximum extension of the baton passer's arm as well as that of the receiver at the instant of exchange (Figures 16a and 16b). They explain the discard-

Figure 16a

NORTH CAROLINA STATE
RELAY TEAM PREPARING
TO EXCHANGE BATON.

Figure 16b

NORTH CAROLINA STATE
RELAY TEAM PRACTICING
PASS. SEE "FREE SPACE."

ing of the former favorite, the hand-on-hip reception, as not efficient in its use of "free space." They point out that the receiver loses the advantage of full extension of his arm backward even though the in-coming runner may achieve full extension of his. If the pass using maximum extension of the arms of both runners is efficiently completed, there can be no doubt that the receiver will get the baton sooner than with the hand-on-hip style. So much attention is being given to matters like maximum use of free space that some coaches are forgetting that the use of *maximum speed* of both runners during the exchange is of far greater significance. You might ask yourself, "In how many sprint relays in the past year have I seen two runners make use of free space without either the in-coming runner being overextended in his effort to reach the receiver or the out-going runner having to slow down to let his teammate catch him?" Even if the exchange was made with both runners stretching to their maximum, did this compensate for the loss of speed on the part of either runner? By far the worst problem in the sprint relay seems to me to be the timing of the exchange so that each runner is going his fastest when the pass is made. I suppose that all of us are dreaming of the ideal pass in which four great sprinters combine their top efforts with three perfect passes, using every inch of free space. Certainly we should all be trying for the ideal even with our less-than-record-breaking high school or college teams, but we may need to emphasize other factors much more than the use of free space. The ideal is rarely achieved.

To point out the truth of what I contend, I refer you to the sprint relay race between the Americas and Europe in the Expo 57 track meet. Here we had a world's record holding U.S. sprint relay team racing a fine European team. The U.S. team lost the race in less than world record time. But it was not the failure to use free space efficiently that caused the defeat; it was primarily the poor timing of the exchange between the last two runners of the U.S. team. Pictures of the exchange show definitely that the outgoing runner had to slow down and turn partially toward the incoming runner to get the baton within the zone. Meanwhile, the European team had completed a pass with fair but certainly not maximum use of the free space, but nevertheless with good speed in the exchange and no loss of momentum by the outgoing runner. I certainly agree that we should coach for good usage of the free space in any relay exchange, but I think that most of us with our mediocre high school or college teams must try to eliminate the more harmful weaknesses. If you are the coach who has that relay team that can challenge the world's record, by all means work on every phase of the exchange that can help your team to gain the tenths of seconds that are so meaningful.

When I see the frequent use of the *inside pass* in all types of relay racing today, I cannot help recalling the many questions raised by coaches when only a few were trying it out about 25 years ago. At that time, George Eastment, then coach of Manhattan College, was a firm believer in its efficiency while I myself had tried it out rather successfully and had written an article on its use for *Scholastic Coach Magazine*. We had some trouble convincing other coaches that anything but the traditional left to right pass was worth considering. I doubt that either George or I was the first to use the pass, but it was interesting to see the swing toward its use that followed the appearance of our recommendations of it. Perhaps more significant to you as a coach is the fact that much of what I wrote in that *Scholastic Coach* article still holds as an assessment of the strengths and weaknesses of that same *inside pass*. There are a few instances in which the inside pass is dangerous to use, but there are still many occasions when it should be employed. Since the days when only a few of us were urging its use, others have gone beyond us and introduced the alternating passes, some inside and some outside in the same race as conditions warrant their use.

Let's consider first the advantages of the right-to-left pass. Obviously the man receiving it will be turned toward the pole position as he receives the baton, not turned toward the right as he is in using the left-to-right pass. He gains a half-step advantage upon an opponent using the traditional pass by not having to turn his body back toward the pole (Figure 17). If

Photo by Don Wilkinson

Figure 17

LEE EVANS PASSING TO TOMMY SMITH, SAN JOSE STATE.

he is in one of the outside lanes, this can help him to cut for the pole immediately. Assuming other things to be equal, this means that three successful inside passes will give your team a step and a half advantage over the team not using it. This is worth gaining.

The inside pass is not without its dangers, however. If your team has the pole position on a track that has a wall or a fence close to the inside of the track, the runner coming in can have trouble. Since he is passing with his right hand to his teammate's left, he will often be heading toward the inside of the track and can crash into the fence or wall. I have seen this happen several times and the runners rather badly shaken by the collision. In such a situation, I would not use an inside pass.

PLACING MEN FOR EFFECT

Every coach is concerned about his team's loss of speed during a baton exchange. Too often he sees his incoming runner catch and sometimes pass the outgoing runner before completing the exchange. Again he may see his receiver start too soon and spoil the exchange by having to slow down or even stop to get the baton within the zone. What can the coach do to help his relay team lessen the danger of poor timing and consequent loss of speed in the exchange? Actually, both the failure of the incoming man to catch his receiver and the by-passing of his receiver at the time of the exchange can stem from the same fault—the starting signal for the outgoing man may be off. Though some relay teams use a voice signal to set the receiver in motion, most use a visual signal for the outgoing runner to start. When the vocal signal is used, it is frequently given by the incoming runner, who will shout, "Go!" or some similar word when he believes he is within good passing range. Some coaches prefer this type of signal to that of setting a mark which the outgoing runner will use to signal his start the instant that his teammate reaches it. Still other coaches teach the combination of a vocal signal and a visual one.

The danger with the vocal signal is that in the excitement of close baton exchanges, several other runners and sometimes spectators are shouting and can drown out the important signal of the man coming in. There is also a tendency on the part of the incoming runner to fear that he may give the call too soon and be unable to catch his speeding team mate. This often results in the passer's catching his man before the latter can get up speed. Poor exchanges and even fumbling of the baton are frequent results of this error. One advantage of the vocal signal is that it does enable a tiring runner to take another stride or so before he sets the receiver in motion. If you like the vocal signal for your team then you should set up a word signal that will be short and distinctive and not likely to be shouted by anyone but your own runners.

At times the vocal signal itself is not at fault. The receiver sometimes is watching his approaching team mate, and after getting the starting signal, *then* turns and starts his sprint. This often means the fractional time loss between the signal and the take-off which leads to the poor exchange. Still another consideration must be the quick build-up of speed on the part of the receiver. Whether the starting signal be vocal or visual, the outgoing man *must* get up as much speed as possible once he starts to move. It has been my observation that more faulty baton passes result from the failure of the outgoing runner to get up enough speed than from any other cause. In putting together his relay team, the coach needs to give a great deal of thought to the relative speeds of the passer and receiver. If possible, he should have the two working together many, many times. He must impress upon both runners the necessity of completing the exchange with both runners at top speed or as close to top speed as they can get.

Coaches who favor the visual type of signal for the outgoing runner sometimes have their boys set up a mark on or at the side of the track. The receiver watches this mark until his team mate reaches it and then goes, attempting to build up speed as quickly as he can. What some coaches neglect in setting up these marks with their boys is to emphasize that such a mark must be governed by the ability of the outgoing runner to build up speed rapidly. Just how much leeway the receiver needs can be determined only after constant practice, allowing the two runners to become accustomed to each other. The big danger with the visual starting signal is that the outgoing runner will be watching that mark and starting when it is reached, often without observing the condition of the incoming man. If that man is tiring or is jostled, the receiver often has to ease up to avoid going out of the passing zone before his team mate can catch him. The coach should also notice whether the boy receiving has a tendency to be over-eager and start too soon. I have seen this error result in many a bad exchange. When the coach juggles his men so that the receiver is not familiar with the speed of the incoming runner, he should check very carefully in practice to correct any such mistake by the man awaiting the baton.

Like many another high school coach, I have had to juggle my relay team and its order frequently. The need of doubling in the regular sprints has often led to my having to substitute for a regular member of the relay team. It is for this reason that I often have six or seven boys practicing baton exchanges. I also think it wise to interchange them so that they will have some knowledge of the speed of any runner who might be inserted in an emergency. I do this more often than many other coaches, I have noticed. This does not mean, however, that I do not spend plenty of time with the four sprinters who are likely to be my top team.

USING THE "TAKE CHARGE" MAN

Because I interchange team members frequently, I like to have my runners use a combination of vocal and visual signals. They will have a pre-established mark set as a starting signal, but especially in the 880 relay I have the incoming runner who finds himself in trouble ready to shout some word like "Red!" just before he reaches the mark so that the receiver is warned not to take off too soon. Upon hearing that signal, the outgoing runner waits one more stride and then takes off, still trying to reach top speed quickly. I prefer having the outgoing runner wait till the incoming man has taken one more stride to having him go out more slowly. I want all exchanges to be at the best speed possible.

Because I feel so strongly about the need of making all baton exchanges at top speed, I very seldom allow my relay team members to practise at half speed or three-quarter speed. Only when I am trying to illustrate an exchange point do I let the boys work at less than racing speed. I do not insist upon their running the full distance of the leg, but enough of it to get them going very fast (Figure 18).

You may have seen occasional experiments by coaches in an effort to improve their team's passing in sprint relays. Several of these are worth some study. At times a coach will place his receiver not at the beginning of the passing zone or in the sprint area preceding it but well into the zone; sometimes even half way through the zone. This bit of racing tactics can under some circumstances pay off. It is used by some coaches to allow a very fast man to carry the baton the maximum distance before delivering it to a much slower man. It is also used by some coaches in races in which runners exchanging the batons are likely to be very close and in tight quarters. The coach therefore will have his incoming runner sprint past the usual exchange area to pass the baton while clear of the pack. Such an arrangement allows the outgoing man very little space in which to get up speed and to receive the baton. However, it can be helpful in avoiding the area of mass exchange and the resultant danger of dropping batons. I would be careful not to use such a plan if the teams were not required to hold their passing lanes. If the receivers are permitted to move to the pole as their team mates approach the passing zone, I am afraid of the obstruction of my incoming man by others trying to rush into position at the pole. The coach should weigh the advantages and disadvantages carefully in such a situation.

Though coaches as a rule are upset when they see one of their boys actually pass a receiver in the passing zone, some might be interested in

Track and Field News

Figure 18

HENRY CARR TAKES THE BATON FOR THE FINAL LEG OF THE 1964
OLYMPIC 1600 METER RELAY.

an experimental type of pass that I saw a prominent Argentine coach testing out recently. It is quite the reverse of the usual passing pattern. The receiver was set in starting position and the incoming runner passed him, going into the relay zone. As his team mate passed, the receiver started his sprint. The incoming man continued at full speed and then held the baton up for his team mate to grasp as he sped past. The receiver simply took the baton from the hand of the first runner as they were side by side. If you are the experimental type of coach, try that one out. It may have real possibilities.

PREPARING FOR THE DISTANCE AND MEDLEY RELAYS

One look at the program of any of the big relay carnivals on either the high school or the college level or at any of the big winter indoor meets is all that any coach needs to convince himself of the popularity of the mile relay. An occasional medley or two-mile relay is inserted for variety, but from Boston to Los Angeles, the mile relay is a glamour event. For this reason, it seems to me, it becomes an easier event for motivation than many others. In the usual competition, the mile relay does not demand the great speed needed in sprint relays nor the intense background work of the mile itself. This is not to say that training for the quarter mile is easy. Far from it! But since the mile relay involves quarter milers, it retains some of the natural appeal of the sprint events, and, in the eyes of the schoolboy, less of the drudgery he associates with long distance running. The high school boy with only moderate speed still eyes the quarter mile as the event within his reach. The coach has several things working in his favor. Besides the boy's willingness to tackle a middle distance rather than a long distance run, the coach can suggest the possibility of his making the mile relay team. If trips to such meets as the Penn or Drake Relays or any of the other great relay carnivals are scheduled for his team, the coach has an added and very powerful means of motivation. More than that, he also knows that since the 440 demands endurance as well as some speed, he can set up a training schedule that will help the boy to reach his goal.

One of the ways to arouse the boy's interest in the mile relay, or for that matter in the 440, is to have him check his speed for the 220. Even though his time for the 220 will make it evident that he has no great hope of making the 880 relay team, it may often be good enough to indicate possibilities for the quarter mile. I am not talking now about national championship calibre relay talent but about quarter milers who make up literally thousands of high school and even college relay teams all across the country. Remember that all it takes to break 3:30 in the mile relay is a couple of 52-second quarter milers paired with a couple of 53-second quarter milers. It is relatively easy to make an aspiring mile relay candidate understand that even though he may have to go all out to hit 24 seconds in the 220 around a turn, the 52- or 53-second quarter is still well within his reach if he wants to work for it.

The coach should be wise enough to capitalize on the boy's natural interest in being one of the team. Indeed, he should notice that his relay team members become a rather closely knit unit. Used wisely, this tendency can work in the coach's favor as well as in the athlete's. Indeed, this very cohesiveness is just what the coach should strive for in preparing his relay teams. He should be aware that this is a natural inclination among boys and that he has only to build it up to achieve effective motivation.

Certain other aspects of this interesting attitude of boys toward their relay teams deserve attention. Although most boys can be caught up in team spirit that runs through any good, well coached squad, there is something a little special about the feeling that binds the members of a relay team. Curiously enough, I have found that it is especially evident among the boys who make up the mile relay team. Don't ask me why. I don't know, unless it is that they see the event as a *small* team effort which can afford the success that the team as a whole may not enjoy. I have noticed that even when the track team is having only fair success in competition, there seems to be a little different feeling among those who make up the relay team. In a strange way, it seems a little different from the selfish attitude of the boy who is satisfied to win his event whether the team wins or not. It actually carries a little of the team spirit that the coach is seeking in his squad as a whole. The coach should be quick to encourage this attitude.

The mile relay group can be shaped into a cohesive unit fairly easily, once the coach has the members working together frequently. Since each runner is covering the same relative distance in his leg, there is likely to be an interesting mixture of individual competition and team pride. You have only to listen in as the members of your relay team chat together, half-challenging and half-encouraging each other before a race. Then notice how the four rush together after a winning effort. The four runners are congratulating each other, sputtering enthusiastically about their comparative times, kidding the team member who made the win a little tougher, and hugging the one who made the big move that ensured the victory. No doubt what I have observed about the mile relay squad can be pointed out about other relay teams just as easily. From school to school the glamour event may differ, but the coach is wise to grasp the opportunity offered. Here is one of the strong motivating factors almost ready-made for the coach to use. The spirit, the friendly rivalry within the group, and the pride of accomplishment can be used to generate the enthusiasm that can sweep through the whole squad and lift it to greater achievements than it dreamed possible. But the coach should never forget that this all starts with the encouragement of the four individuals to reach personal goals and then contribute to the success of the "team within the team."

What has been said about the use of the mile relay team in the motivation of individuals can be applied to the group who make up the two-mile team or any medley relay. I have found that an enthusiastic coach can work from the build-up of what might be called "competitive pride" among the members of a relay group to the inspiration of the track team as a whole. The spirit is catching, provided that the coach is quick to take advantage of it.

Once the mile relay team and its alternates have been established, it can obviously be helped toward success by the coach's manipulation of the personnel that he has available. If the coach is alert, he should soon recognize important differences among the team members. In any of the distance relays, the placement of the runners is a very important consideration, perhaps even a little more important than in the sprint relays. I say this because the misplacement of a runner in any of the distance relays can lead to a much greater loss of yardage than in the shorter relays. For that reason, let's take a very close look at the individuals who make up any mile or two-mile team. All of us have seen runners who look great while they are streaking along in front of the pack, but who seconds later fold badly when someone passes. Quite often the coach is tempted to blast such a runner for his failure by calling him a quitter or gutless. I don't like to use such terms to my runners because I am convinced that often what causes them to fold is *actually their effort* to hold off or stay with the man challenging. This results in the tension and tightness that defeats their purposes. When a coach knows that one of his runners has this tendency to tie up badly under sudden pressure, he will be wise to arrange his relay team in such a way that this runner may receive the baton with a good lead. This may mean that the coach will use his best man first against lead-off men who may be somewhat inferior. He will need to impress on this top man the need of building up as big a lead as possible. Should he be unable to do so, the move may backfire, but with the weak man to protect, the coach can do little else.

PUTTING PRESSURE ON OPPONENTS

If there are two other good runners on the team, the coach should run his weak man second and give the other two a shot at making up ground if their teammate weakens. The only other possibility seems to me to be to run the weak man at anchor. I realize that he will be likely to be against the top men of their other teams, but it is possible that your top three men can give him a lead that he can hold. If I decided to run him on the second leg, I would probably try one more move to assist him. If this happened to be the mile relay, I would urge him to go out very fast for the first 70 or 80 yards after receiving the baton. In high school relay racing this can pay off because it will often open up an even bigger gap between him and the field when he gets a lead from the first man. Most high school runners get a bit panicky in such situations and try to make up the ground too quickly. They will often try to cut down the entire lead in the first 220 yards and leave themselves with little reserve for the final drive to the passing zone. The weak man on your team is thus helped since the challenge that tightens him up so badly is not so likely to come. His challengers may well have spent themselves trying to cut down the lead too early in the race.

In planning the various medley relays, the coach should realize that it is the men running the long distances in these relays that are the key men. Though the runners handling the 220 legs can be of assistance if they outclass the others opposed to them, they cannot be of great help if they are merely the equals of other 220 men in the race. If you know that your 220 man is a couple of seconds faster than the others in the field, it may be worth the gamble to use him in this leg of a medley relay but it is the half miler and the miler in the medley relays who must be good. When I put a good 220 man into a medley relay, I talk to him in terms of the second or two seconds that he must beat his rivals by, not so much about the distance he must lead. I try to make him see his part in the race as a *contribution of protective time* to his teammate running the distance leg of the race. This may prevent him from easing up when he finds himself with a seemingly comfortable lead. All of us have seen good half milers and milers cut down what looked like impossible margins in relay races. While I may work on runners handling the sprint leg of the medley in such fashion, I use a different approach with those on the distance legs. I make it very clear to them that they must avoid the temptation to go out wildly after an opponent who takes the baton with a substantial lead. I try to point out to them the wisdom of cutting down the lead gradually, seeing the margin in terms of yardage to be made up during stages of the race. For example, if my half miler finds himself back 30 yards when he gets the baton, I try to make him see this as something to be cut down by ten yards in each 220 so that he will be closing in on his opponent with the last 220 to be run. It seems to help to point out to your distance runner a ten-yard zone marked off on the football field to make him realize how short this distance really is. If he has this picture in his mind, he is not so likely to make that dramatic first-quarter rush that so often fizzles. I talk to the miler running the distance medley race the same way, pointing out to him that he has four full laps to cut down what may seem like a long lead.

Another type of relay that is being introduced to more and more carnivals is the shuttle hurdle relay. The coach who hopes to do anything in the shuttle hurdles can do much to prepare his team by using the type of interval work with hurdlers that I have mentioned in my earlier chapter on working with hurdlers. By using the football field lines and facing hurdles both ways, he can have his team of hurdlers working just as they will be in the actual race. I have found that running endless relays over hurdles is just as effective as the method is in working with regular runners. The hurdlers merely change ends of the field each leg and continue their hurdling with the last hurdler just moving quickly over to the starting line to run the second leg. This gives him a little more recovery time than he would have if he had to start on the first leg immediately. The reversing of the starting and finishing lines still leaves him with less recovery time than the number two man, but you can vary this by switching him to a different leg if you wish. This is good work for all hurdlers but especially valuable if you are planning to enter a team in the shuttle hurdles relay.

	WORKING
Chapter	**WITH SELF-DRIVING**
5	**WEIGHT MEN**

Among all of the competitors in track and field, none hold a more paradoxical reputation than those who throw the weights, whether they be shot putters, hammer throwers, discus throwers, or javelin throwers. Variously described as "muscle men," "hardware heavers," or "metal movers," they are almost without exception a truly dedicated group of athletes. Frequently clannish and somewhat aloof, they are often kidded unmercifully by their teammates and others. Big men of track that they usually are, they take pride in their size and strength and often go through little rituals of their own, literally trying to "psyche" themselves into readiness for that explosive effort so characteristic of their events. Almost without exception, they spend hours working with weights to build up more strength. Once caught up in the spirit of their event, they are likely to go to great lengths to reach the goals they desire. Many become so interested in their sport that they will set up their own throwing circles or areas at home, and own their own implements and sets of weights. Once bitten by the weight bug, they need little or no motivation and may even have to be checked from throwing too much rather than prodded for throwing too little. Truly, they are a breed in themselves. I say this not in any derogatory sense but to remind the coach that these men, like the distance runners, *drive themselves*. Often they receive far less attention from the coach than they deserve.

HANDLING THE IMPLEMENTS CORRECTLY

Unlike sprinters, they can build up the necessary speed involved in their events, whether shot, hammer, or discus throwing. Only the javelin throw makes demands upon natural talent, i.e. a great throwing arm. But it will not take any coach long to find out that size alone is not the real answer to shot putting, hammer throwing, or discus throwing. The big man without coordination is not a good weight man. Like many of the giants playing professional football and basketball today, the weight man in track must have both speed and coordination. For evidence of this, you need only look at Randy Matson, outstanding in both shot and discus but also talented enough to make a starting berth on his college's basketball team. Most important for the coach to remember, however, is the fact that weight training programs can build average bodies into strong and powerful ones; coordination can be improved with constant practice; and speed enough to suffice for the weight events can be developed. Though the great javelin throwers are those with strong throwing arms, the coach can help those with only average arms to achieve some success in their event.

It is perhaps not so surprising that boys of high school age and men are not too difficult to interest in the weight events. It seems part of the nature of man to take pride in a well-developed body that enables him to perform feats of strength. Even the legends of primitive people are filled with the stories of the man of super strength. Each has its Hercules, its Paul Bunyan, its mover of mountains. Feats of strength like tossing the caber and throwing the heavy weight have for centuries been a part of the contests that pit men against each other. This is the point that the track coach should keep in mind when he tries to interest candidates in trying the weight events and later in motivating them to accept the long hours of practice necessary for success. Many a young high school boy too big and awkward to have any hope of success in distance running and a little too slow to get very far in the sprints can be steered into the weight events if the coach is shrewd enough to capitalize on man's natural pride in his strength. What is most satisfying is that once caught up in this desire to perform feats of strength, the boy often becomes self motivating. All around him he can see others who have built scrawny bodies into strong and powerful ones. It is no accident that the ads playing up the boy's secret wish to become strong and muscular have drawn thousands of letters and sold thousands of implements.

CONCENTRATION OF EFFORT IN FRACTIONAL TIME

When the coach has persuaded boys to try out for the weight events such as the shot put or discus throw, he next faces a problem that is slightly different from that involved in any phase of the running events except starting in the sprints. Indeed, though there is some resemblance between the drive off the starting blocks and the explosive effort at the instant of release of the shot, there can be no correction of an error made in the release of shot, hammer, discus, or javelin. A faulty start in the sprints may possibly be offset by extra effort in the race, but once the implement thrown leaves the hand there can be no second chance with *that* particular throw. The only saving grace in the field events is the multiple trials allowed.

It has been quite interesting to me to talk with several field event coaches from foreign countries who are quite critical of the discus-throwing techniques of some of our best men. On the other hand, I have seldom heard much criticism of the form of our best shot putters. Our leading javelin throwers and hammer throwers also come in for fairly frequent criticism. The comment usually is that we in the United States are placing too much emphasis upon developing great strength in our field event men without giving equal attention to perfection of technique. I have noticed, however, that in recent months the foreign coaches are also beginning to insist upon more and more weight training in their efforts to compete with athletes like Randy Matson and others of our powerful young shot-putting clan. It has been my observation too that some of the European and South American field event coaches are so wrapped up in their insistence upon perfect form in the field events that they overlook another very necessary factor, the determination to win. Perhaps we United States coaches may go a bit overboard in our emphasis upon winning, but I don't think so. It puzzles me to consider why we are competing if we are not disturbed by losing. I realize that the old clichés about being a good loser are common, but I notice that they are the comments made to the man *after he has lost*. They are, in other words, *the consolation prize*. While the athlete is in the thick of the competition, I don't notice anyone, foreign or domestic, teammate, coach or spectator, shouting for him to lose. The determination to win is as much a part of the make-up of a champion as his technique and at times it can cause him to rise above his mistakes.

THE BUILD-UP OF IMPLEMENT SPEED

But let me not be misunderstood about the importance of technique in field events. Perhaps it is time that we coaches in the United States began to reassess our ideas about the form we seek in our field events. The tremendous advances in the shot put came about only after men like Jim Fuchs of Yale and Parry O'Brien began to think seriously about ways of applying leverage to the shot over a longer line than was possible in the old style, starting with the left side toward the toe board. Now hardly a good athlete in the world throws the shot with any other form than the so-called O'Brien style or some slight variation of it. Discus throwers began passing the 200-foot mark not only after they had begun to use weight training but also after they began to sweep the discus over a longer area than had previously been used. Danek not only has tremendous leg strength but has worked incessantly upon the perfection of a rhythmic progression across the circle that is highly efficient and successful. It may be worthwhile for us coaches here to study the differences between Danek's style and that of our own athletes.

Lately it has pleased me to observe that United States coaches have been giving much more attention to javelin-throwing technique. Especially on the high school level there has been much progress made. More and more high school javelin throwers are getting beyond the 200-foot mark and quite a few are passing the 225-foot line. This progress has been the result of strength development, but strength development coupled with more careful study of the technique of the event. It has been refreshing to note the attention being given by both coach and athlete to the cross-over leading to the delivery. Here the emphasis upon rhythmic action at high speed is bringing better and better results.

SECURING CONTROLLED SPEED

As we coaches look at our shot putters and discus throwers, we may be making the same mistake that we make with our sprinters. We may be impressed by what seem to be the outward signs of great effort. We may be delighted by that explosive effort that the weight thrower makes at the instant of release. Yet is it not true that when the shot putter or discus thrower makes his best throws he is talking about how easily he moved the implement? He is saying that the shot felt "light in his hand" or that the discus seemed to fly off his hand without that tug that gave the feeling of force exerted upon it. Perhaps it is in this comment that we should be seeing the clue to our future work on technique in the throwing events. This is not to say that there should be no conscious effort at the instant of release in the put or throw. On the contrary, it should come as the climax of a rhythmic build-up of power, starting with the lift from the legs at the end of fast, well-balanced motion across the circle. The lift from the legs should continue with the muscles of the back taking up the drive and then with the extension of the throwing arm, and should end with the flip of the wrist that sends the shot on its way.

One of the most discouraging things for a beginning shot putter to experience is to suffer the strain of having the full weight of the shot resting upon his fingers because he has tried to complete the push on the shot before his legs, back, and arms have done their work. He should be cautioned against starting the delivery of the shot too soon. If he tries to get his wrist flip in prematurely, he is likely to find his fingers bent backward very painfully. While your shot putter is learning the event, you will do well to avoid stressing the wrist flip, but instead, emphasize the *wait* with the shot until the legs and back have done their work. You should realize that this is difficult for the beginner to do. He is usually too intent upon getting rid of the shot. The result is often a sore arm and sometimes sprained wrist or fingers. Beginners need plenty of practice getting the feel of letting the legs do their work in the lifting of the shot. Their tendency to try to throw the shot and the consequent arm strain that usually follows will be a challenge to the coach's ability to motivate the candidate and bring him through this rather discouraging stage of shot putting.

THE PROBLEM OF BALANCE

In working with beginners in both the shot put and the discus throw, the coach is unwise to put too much emphasis on speed across the circle. Many times I have heard coaches hammering away at what they consider the boy's inadequate speed, but what they were overlooking was the boy's inability to handle what limited speed he was using and still keep in good balance. Speed uncontrolled in the shot put movement across the circle or in the rotation within the discus circle is practically useless. It is poor motivation on the coach's part to keep insisting upon speed and more speed before the boy has learned what it means to throw on balance. Only after the athlete has the feeling of moving in balance and coming to the power position in both shot and discus should he be expected to try for an increase in speed across the circle (Figures 19 and 20).

Some coaches also make the mistake of thinking that the use of the hips in the delivery of the shot and that of the discus are alike. In shot putting, the right leg drives hard as soon as the right foot is back on the ground firmly after the initial glide. The drive of the leg should *lift* the right hip *before* it starts to rotate toward the front. Rotation of the hip too early kills the lift so important in getting the legs under the shot.

The discus thrower, on the other hand, *should* start the rotation of the hip immediately when the right foot is down. Whether the coach is working with a beginning shot putter or a beginning discus thrower, it is very important that he clarify this difference in the techniques of the two events.

Figure 19

JOHN DRISCOLL OF MELROSE HIGH SCHOOL—NEW ENGLAND H.S. CHAMPION.

Figure 20

DALLAS LONG OF SOUTHERN CALIFORNIA.

SC Photo

In coaching the shot put, the coach must realize that his efforts to help his beginners must be based upon the gradual perfection of a technique based upon the following principles. The *shot* must pick up speed as it moves across the circle and be travelling at *maximum* speed at the instant of release. The putter must deliver the final push to the shot from as far back and as low as possible so that he can make full use of the large leg and back muscles. The lesser muscles of shoulder and arm should not be brought into the action too soon. One of the big mistakes in shot putting is that of starting the shot delivery too soon. Ironically, this usually results from the boy's over-eagerness to push the shot. He is often moving so fast that he fails to let the leg and back muscles do their full job. (See Figure 21.)

Figure 21

STEINHAUER, U.S.A.—PAN AM GAMES.

Photo by Don Wilkinson

WHAT FOULING REVEALS

Good shot putting also involves the build up of speed in a straight line as well as in balance. The shot putter should realize that the very limited circle in which he must work has hindered his attempt to exert force. If he does not move in a straight line across the circle, he does not make use of even the limited area to which he is entitled. The most flagrant and perhaps the most common error is that of letting the left foot fall too far left of center, leaving the putter in a very weak position. He may be compared with the baseball batter who loses most of his hitting power when he drops his front foot "in the bucket." His left foot falls so far out of line that all he can do is to punch the ball weakly to the opposite field. The shot putter who drops his front foot too far to the left of center is making the same mistake. He has left himself in a very weak power position. Quite often the coach will notice that after the shot leaves the putter's hand, the boy will foul by falling out of the circle on the left side. Obviously his body is not under the shot but is falling away from it.

In attempting to correct such a fault, the coach should emphasize that this is almost always the result of the boy's starting the rotation of his hips too early. Often he is starting the right hip rotation even before his left foot has a chance to touch the ground. Because his left foot is still in the air, it swings much farther to the left than it should before he can plant it. Another clue to aid the coach in spotting this fault is the boy's head. His head, instead of remaining quite still until the lift of the right leg is complete, will actually lead the body in its rotational movement. This can be corrected by having the boy fix his eyes directly on some spot or object outside the rear of the circle and try to keep that mark in sight as long as possible. (See Figure 22.)

When the coach notices his shot putter getting too many of his puts off to the right of center, he should notice whether the boy is doing the opposite of putting his foot "in the bucket." He may well be keeping that left foot so close to the center of the circle that he is blocking the movement of his right hip as he lifts and then starts it forward. The left foot must fall just slightly to the left of an imaginary center line to allow the right side to come through without being blocked. If the coach plays golf he may remember the pro's instruction to him to turn the toes of his left foot slightly to the left to allow his club a chance to follow through without being blocked by his left side. Though there is not complete agreement about the use of the left leg in the shot put, it seems to me that for

Figure 22

MATSON, U.S.A., DISCUS THROWING—PAN AM GAMES.

Photo by Don Wilkinson

a good follow-through the same principle must hold. What the coach is really looking for in the shot put is to have his boy move that shot from as low as possible through as long a plane as possible, building up speed as he moves and keeping hand contact with that shot until he has exerted every bit of force upon it, and then saving himself from being propelled out of the circle *directly behind the shot*.

An important factor often overlooked in the shot putter's immediate preparation for his effort is the need of concentration. Many shot putters waste trials by making only half-hearted efforts in their first one or two puts. They place the shot very casually in their hand and as a result have it slide off their fingers in the act of putting, or they start their motion across the circle while still poorly balanced. There is little to be gained by a fine preliminary glide and excellent balance at the instant of delivery if the shot then slides weakly off the fingers. The athlete should be taught to concentrate fully on each phase of his putting, *beginning with the correct placement of the shot in his hand*. This should be done in practice as well as in the meet, as careless mistakes in practice can do no good.

Perhaps even more frequent is the mistake of starting the putting action while not in balance. The shot putter who is leaning too far forward as he starts his motion finds it almost impossible to get in balance as he

113

moves across the circle. There should be great concentration at this point because so much depends upon direction, speed, and balance in the glide. The boy should never start his glide whether in practice or in a meet without full concentration upon his effort. If he feels uncomfortable or slightly off balance, he should stop immediately and pull himself together for another attempt. To go through with the trial carelessly is throwing away one of the three tries that he has. I have pounded upon this point with my field event men time after time. The athlete in the field events, unless he makes the finals, has to deliver his best in one of three attempts. It will do him no good at all to walk into the circle ten minutes later and get off a toss that is several feet farther than the one that won the competition.

HANDLING INDIVIDUAL'S TENSIONS

All of us coaches have run into what horse racing trainers call a "morning-glory." In horse racing, he is the horse that looks great in an early morning workout but gets nowhere in the race. It is a mighty trying experience for the coach to see his shot putter or discus thrower getting off great throws in practice and then folding badly during meets. Such athletes are real problems. One of the most interesting books that I have come upon recently is *Problem Athletes and How to Handle Them* by Dr. Bruce Ogilvie and Dr. Thomas A. Tutko. This is a study well worth the reading.

I have tried many ways to get the "morning-glory" athlete to deliver in a meet, and on some occasions I have been successful. One of the methods I use is to have the athlete work in practice sessions exactly as though he were competing in a meet. I make him take his practice throws in sets of three, insisting that he concentrate upon getting away a measured throw among each three. At times I have him competing with other shot putters from his own team. In other words I do all I can to simulate the conditions under which he will be competing. If he is a moaner, I will make him use a type of shot that he dislikes so that he will forget his complaints about the implements he will have to use during the meet. Sometimes the method works. The boy becomes so used to working under meet conditions that he loses his fears and manages to get off some good puts or throws. I wish that I could tell you that the method always works. It doesn't, but it has worked often enough to give me some faith in it. I suggest that you give it a try if you face this exasperating problem.

In working with discus throwers, the coach will often find that trouble can stem from the same sources that bother his young shot putters. They too are likely to be rather careless in gripping the discus, and unless frequently reminded of it they spoil throws by letting the discus slip off the side of their hands or hold the discus too tightly so that it flips over and over with worthless wobbling flights resulting. Here again the coach will be wise to insist upon the thrower's complete concentration upon each phase of his effort. This should begin with his attention to the placement of the discus in his hand with fingers well spread, especially if he has rather small hands. He should be warned to guard against gripping the discus too tightly, while at the same time being sure that he has the implement under full control.

With young throwers, the coach should stress the need of making every effort a worthwhile one whether it be a practice throw for correcting some fault or a throw in competition. I want my discus throwers and, for that matter, all of my field event men, to be all business when they work out and when they compete. I see no value at all in slipshod practices. I like to put my discus thrower, among others, on a spot. I may say to the boy, "You have just this throw left and it will decide the meet. What are you going to do with it?" I confess that I don't let him take the challenge very lightly. If he goes about his preparation carelessly, I will give him a pretty good tongue lashing. I don't hesitate to remind him that such an attitude in a real meet could undo the fine efforts of a score of his teammates. If I notice that he goes about his effort deliberately and makes a real effort to get the discus out there, I will be just as quick to praise him, regardless of how poor the resulting throw may be. My feeling is that if he will work that hard on a practice throw, the time will not be far off when the throws will be good ones. If they are not, the fault may well be mine, not his.

The coach working with his beginning discus throwers will often make the same mistake he makes with beginning shot putters. He is so anxious to see his discus thrower get speed into his turns that he overlooks some of the very factors that detract from that speed or at any rate from the length of the resulting throw. I am sure that any coach who knows his business will be quick to correct one of the most common faults in beginning discus throwers, that of releasing the discus from the back of the hand so that the discus rotates in the opposite way from the correct one and goes nowhere. It is surprising how many boys start this way and must be corrected. Nevertheless, I have seen and heard coaches ranting about the lack of speed across the circle while overlooking the most obvious fault in the book.

Strictly speaking, the athlete does not really *throw* the discus (Figure 23). Very seldom today do we see a young boy using an old-fashioned sling to throw rocks. He is not likely to be acquainted with the sensation

Photo by Don Wilkinson

Figure 23

STOCKER, U.S.A.—LOS ANGELES TIMES INTERNATIONAL MEET.

of swinging a rock held in the leather pocket of little David's legendary weapon. He may not really understand what you mean when you tell him to "sling" the discus. Yet that is just what he must do. He must think of his arm as the thongs of the sling and his hand as somewhat like the leather pocket holding a rock. His arm must be fully extended and the discus swept around in as wide an arc as possible and kept behind his legs until he reaches the power position and whips the discus on its way. The motion is not a natural one for the American boy who is so used to throwing a baseball in a very different manner. It may be worthwhile to remind you here that your understanding of the importance of the discus thrower's fully extended arm will make it clear to you why the discus thrower with unusually long arms is often a fine prospect. Since the height at which the discus is released has some effect upon the distance of its flight (other things being equal) you can see why the very tall boy with exceptionally long arms is worth your effort to instruct in this event. Don't give up too easily on such a prospect (Figure 24).

Figure 24

OERTER, U.S.A.—LOS ANGELES TIMES INTERNATIONAL MEET.

Photo by Don Wilkinson

THE PSYCHOLOGY OF COMFORT

Let's assume that you have your discus candidate well grounded in the fundamentals of gripping and releasing the discus and sweeping it well out from the body as he builds up speed for the delivery. Now that he feels secure in the circle and moves through his rotation under good control, you may want to help him get more speed in his movement across the circle. This is the time to consider increasing his speed. Don't imagine for an instant that this is something easy. The faster he moves, the faster other things must happen in the technique of the complete effort. Yet he must master the increase in speed without loss of rhythm and body balance.

You can begin your efforts to help the boy increase his speed by having him concentrate first on keeping the knee of his bent right leg held close to his body. This action enables him to rotate faster, and he must be reminded to bring his right foot down rapidly as he drives his body powerfully into the full turn leading to the delivery of the discus. Very few young throwers can master the increase in speed without some sacrifice of rhythm and balance. For a while their distance may decrease. The coach should not let them become discouraged but should remind them that even the greatest discus throwers spend hours trying to perfect their technique. After a while, one or two good throws are bound to come, and with them the boy's realization that controlled speed will give him the distance that he seeks. You as his coach must convince him that working for speed under control will eventually pay dividends (See Figure 25).

COACHING THE JAVELIN THROWERS

Progress in the javelin throw in the United States has always been limited by the very attitude taken toward it in the high schools in many areas of the country. Only the hammer throw is found in fewer high school meets than the javelin throw, and both are rejected as too dangerous. Ironically, any coach who knows the events will tell you that the javelin thrower has far more control over his implement than the discus thrower has over his. It has always seemed strange to me that in this country where we have some of the strongest and most accurate throwing arms in the world we are reluctant to have the javelin in high school meets while on the other hand, in other parts of the world the woman's javelin throw is a common event in meets. Most high school boys would be ashamed to admit that girls might be more accurate than they are in throwing any implement.

As I reflect upon the so-called great danger in the high school javelin

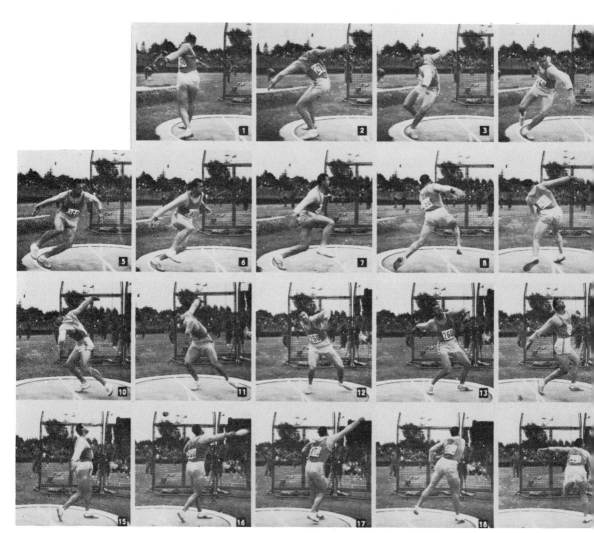

Figure 25

DANEK SEQUENCE—DISCUS THROWING.

throw, I can say truthfully that after seeing literally thousands of boys throw the javelin in practice and in meets, I have seen exactly three persons struck with them, one of them a careless official and the other two, thoughtless competitors. In my years of coaching, I have seen more people struck with the shot than with either discus or javelin. True, the javelin is not something to be thrown without regard for people close to the throwing area, but it is far less likely to go astray than a discus slipping off the hand of a thrower.

The coach who is interested in developing javelin throwers in his school starts by having to combat this attitude in many sections of the country. His job of motivation may start with the school authorities and the parents rather than with the boys on his squad. The boys themselves are easily interesting in trying the event. To reassure any adults who have their doubts about the introduction of the javelin, the wise coach will insist upon practice within restricted areas somewhat removed from those in which other members of his squad are at work. This might seem an unnecessary warning, but unheeded it can cause the very condemnation of the event that has led to its rejection in many states. In addition to assigning the javelin throwers to a restricted area, I would urge the coach to keep their practice supervised and to issue javelins with the understanding that only those boys practicing the event are to touch them. In this way the coach begins his motivation of javelin throwers by teaching the candidates respect for the implement itself. It can be dangerous in the hands of a careless individual, but then so can an automobile.

In looking over his candidates for the event, the coach should realize that he is seeking one thing above all others. There is no substitute for a fine throwing arm for success in the javelin throw. Size and speed help, but they are minor compared with a great arm. The baseball catcher who can really whip that ball down to second base, the pitcher who has that fine overhand fast ball, or the outfielder who can uncork that great overhand throw to the bases is not only the baseball coach's pride and joy; he is the man you want for your javelin thrower. If the boy has the great arm to start with, the good coach can supply the rest; without it he can have only relatively limited success.

Teaching the beginners the correct hand grip on the javelin is every bit as important as teaching the shot putter or the discus thrower how to hold his implement. The boy must be taught that in delivering the javelin he must get a lifting action from the palm of his hand. This is often overlooked and, as a result, the coach and thrower become unhappy about the boy's slow progress. This "up and out" action of the hand in the release of the javelin can be taught to the boy by having him throw short distances, trying to get the feel of this lifting with the palm.

Because the legs are so important in good javelin throwing, it is important to give the boy the feel of having the legs do their work. A stunt I have used frequently to help the boy recognize the feeling of power in his legs is to stand directly behind him grasping the tail of the javelin as he is in throwing position. I then have him go through the throwing motion without actually throwing the javelin but getting the feel of the legs driving forward and upward in the manner that they should in an actual throw.

You may often be bothered by the beginner's tendency to bring the javelin back in such a way that he strikes the ground with the tail of it as he prepares to throw. You should work with him on this point so that he learns to bring the javelin back as far as possible, yet just missing the ground. This error of letting the javelin touch right at the start of the delivery not only weakens the throw but is often responsible for the weird off-direction throws that so frighten those who dislike the event in high school meets.

If you were to ask any good javelin thrower what causes most trouble for beginners in the javelin, I am sure that many would reply that it is the injury to the elbow. To help your candidates to avoid this injury, you will need to remind them constantly that they *must* lead the throw with the elbow. They will also lessen their danger of injury if they do their best to make every throw in good balance, dropping the head slightly to the left to allow the javelin to be brought through directly over the shoulder and very close to the ear (Figure 26). Throws made while off balance cause the back strain that many beginners complain about.

Photo by Joe Sherman, Falmouth, Mass.

Figure 26

FRED ROBINSON OF DENNIS YARMOUTH HIGH SCHOOL—JAVELIN THROW.

You will notice that I have not yet said anything about the approach run or the frequently discussed cross-over steps that precede the delivery. My reason for this is that I think it is rather pointless to start emphasizing the approach run until the boy has fixed clearly in his mind how to execute the cross-over pattern that you intend to have him use, and he has no real need for the cross-over until he has learned the correct delivery of the javelin by throwing it many times without the use of either run or cross-over. Only then do I like to begin work with him, taking him through the cross-over steps slowly and at first without the javelin. Assuming that we will use either the regular front cross-over or the American hop style, I like to have him go through the five basic steps over and over. Using the ten-yard lines on the football field as guides, I like to have the boy move through the pattern more rapidly trying for regularity of stride length. If I find that the boy is having too much trouble with the regular front cross-over pattern and he does not show too much promise as a thrower, I do not hesitate to have him shift to the hop style because American boys seem to fall into this naturally in trying to throw a baseball long distances from the outfield. Watch them sometime and notice how quickly they seem to use the little hop and then a couple of quick steps to get into strong throwing position with a baseball. I know well that the perfectionists in the javelin throw feel that some momentum is lost in the landing from the hop while the front cross-over executed well enables the thrower to continue his forward momentum. Basically, they are right, but many young throwers find the front cross-over difficult to achieve without some loss of balance and a resultant weakened throw. I have found it interesting to use a stop watch to time the thrower's movement through the hop style and through the front cross-over. When both are executed well there is very little indication on a stop watch that any significant speed is gained through the cross-over. Only when the thrower makes his hop too high is there an obvious hesitation when he lands. If he keeps his foot close to the ground and points the toe of the foot slightly to the left as he lands, you will find it hard to detect any loss of momentum as the boy goes into the delivery of the javelin. If you find one of your boys having trouble with the front cross-over and becoming discouraged because of lack of progress, you may give him a big lift by letting him change to the American hop style. Actually he will be concerned with only the hop itself in this pattern as opposed to five steps with the cross-over.

When I am trying to get the boy moving through the steps smoothly, I like to keep things as uncomplicated as possible. I usually want him to do this at first with no javelin to think about, but merely extending his arm backward as if he were carrying the implement. Next I have him carry the javelin and try to coordinate the extension of the throwing arm and the delivery with the step pattern that he is using. I like to have him concentrate on the rhythm, speed and balance of the basic steps and actions leading up to the delivery of the javelin. I may let him throw a few times to learn the feeling of getting his legs into the throw but I do

Photo by Allie Newman,
Cape Cod Standard-Times

Figure 27

ROBINSON—FOLLOW-THROUGH
ON JAVELIN THROW.

Scholastic Coach Magazine

Figure 28

BILL ALLEY, KANSAS—THE JAVELIN THROW.

Figure 29

F. CORVELLI, U.S.A.—THE JAVELIN THROW.

Photo by Don Wilkinson

not want him to try for any great distance. Often I will have him throwing for a cross line on the football field about fifty or sixty feet away. See Figures 27 and 28.

Finally I have the boy use a short approach run, setting up his marks for the beginning of the series of steps involving the cross-over step and the delivery of the javelin. I have him practice the carry of the javelin and its coordination with his approach run, trying to master the coordination of the whole procedure. From that point on it becomes a matter of lengthening the run to his full approach and trying to build up as much speed as he can handle. In my efforts to help him I try to work on one point at a time. If I have been successful in my motivation of the boy, he will be concentrating upon some phase of his event every practice throw he takes from then on (Figure 29).

USING WEIGHT TRAINING AS MOTIVATION

Though some runners today may train without the use of weights, it would be hard to find a shot putter, hammer thrower, discus thrower or javelin thrower who is not using weight training as a vital part of his preparation for his event. The strength needed by any man who hopes to reach championship distances in any of the above named events is amazing. Many who have only limited time in which to practice will devote a greater proportion of that time to working with weights than to practising the event itself. But if you as a coach want to motivate your man effectively, you must not let him put the weight training ahead of the event itself. Young boys especially sometimes become so wrapped up in the weight training program that they forget the purpose for which it is being used. It is important for the coach to know the purpose of each exercise that he has the boy doing and to do his best to make the boy see the connection between each phase of the training and the event in which he is going to compete.

In setting up a weight training program that will help his athlete to make good progress in his given event, the coach must impress upon him the necessity to work hard and faithfully at the exercises. He must make the athlete understand that even with weight training the body must be given time to develop. Some boys have the mistaken idea that two or three weeks of intensive weight training will produce dramatic results. It is important that the coach make the boy think in terms of long range benefits.

After the coach has prepared his athlete for carrying out a long range program, he (the coach) should ask himself the following questions:

Is the exercise that I have chosen the best one for the muscles involved?
Is the weight recommended too heavy or too light?
Is the exercise developing flexibility as well as strength?
How much time does this program require?
How often do I want the boy to do this training?

If the coach has clear in his own mind the purposes for which the various weight training exercises are intended, he is likely to come up with a training program suited to the individual with whom he is working.

Weight training is now widely used in preparing field event men because it serves three purposes. First, it does develop strength. This end is achieved mainly through the use of heavy weights with few repetitions. Second, it helps develop endurance. The consensus seems to be that this is best done through the use of repetitions with light weights. Third, it develops flexibility when the muscle is worked through a full range of motion. If the coach is well aware of these three purposes of weight training and the ways in which they can be carried out, he is ready to prepare a meaningful training program for his athlete. It would be pointless for me to offer any coach here a full scale training program supposedly suitable for every athlete. This seems to me to be as silly as the idea that any distance runner's training schedule will solve the problems of ambitious youngsters all over the country. A meaningful weight training program is a highly individual thing. It takes the boy where he is and aims from there to what he hopes to be months and even years later.

From careful studies by experts in the field, certain general principles have been established. One of these is that to develop strength the muscle must be exercised using the "overload." Tests have shown that strength seems to be developed best through the use of three sets of from four to eight repetitions. The belief is that the muscle should be exercised to exhaustion for best results. But the coach should be aware that weights which will be correct for one athlete may be far too heavy for another. It is the amount of force that is exerted that is the key to strength development.

Another point that is important for the coach to understand is that the length of time that strength and endurance are maintained seems to be highly correlated with the length of time in which they were created. Thus one can see the lack of wisdom in any "rush" program of weight training. When strength and endurance are firmly established, they seem to carry over from one season to the next so that after a few days of a new season the athlete finds a new level of fitness. Here again is the indication that a long range program should be established for the athlete.

Quite a lot of attention has been focused upon isometric training as a substitute for weight training. The coach should know that the value of isometric training for aiding endurance has been seriously questioned, although indications are that it can aid strength. On the other hand, there is plenty of evidence that weight training aids both strength and endurance.

Keeping in mind the muscles involved in the action of shot putting, the coach should make use of such weight exercises as the following: (1) the clean and press; (2) the alternate press, using heavy dumbbells; (3) squats using heavy weights; (4) pull-overs; (5) sit-ups holding weights behind neck and touching elbow to opposite knee; (6) supine press, setting board so that the angle is that of the shot as it is released.

The discus thrower would use the same basic exercises but add (1) lateral raises; (2) rising on toes carrying weights; (3) discus throw movement holding dumbbell and going through the turn bringing the dumbbell to shoulder level. A weighted discus strapped to the hand can be employed effectively in this exercise.

The javelin thrower can use the same set of exercises suggested for the shot putter with the addition of (1) lateral raises; (2) part of a javelin attached to pulley weights on gym rack to be raised as the athlete goes through the throwing motion; (3) chinning and rope climbing.

| Chapter 6 | # BUILDING THE CONFIDENCE OF JUMPERS |

IN AN INTERVIEW WITH BOB SALES OF THE *Boston Globe* not long ago, John Thomas in discussing the high jump remarked, "The bar is the thing you have to beat. That is also the thing that defeats you." He might have said the same thing about the pole vault and to a limited degree about the high hurdles, but he was actually pinpointing an important difference between the high jump and many other events in track. Strictly speaking, the high jump and the pole vault pit man against cross bar. The man does not meet his opponents head-on as he does in the races on the track. He must "beat" the cross bar first in order to defeat his opponents. I realize that some will insist that other events do not put opponents directly against each other. They may go on to point out that broad jumpers, shot putters, triple jumpers, hammer throwers, and javelin throwers, like high jumpers and pole vaulters, compete singly in their own limited areas. That is indeed true, yet in all my years of coaching I have never heard quite the same reaction to discus or shot circles as I have to the cross bar in the high jump and to a lesser degree in the pole vault. High jumpers are sometimes called prima donnas by people who think that they take far too much time getting ready to jump. These people have no conception of the difficulty involved in propelling the body seven feet upward in a single jump. The energy expended is terrific. With this in mind, I'd like to remind coaches of certain psychological factors that need attention in the training of high jumpers.

A LOOK AT HIGH JUMPING

First of all, remember that from the very first attempts that boys make to high jump, they think of the *cross bar,* and not the boys they may be jumping against, as the enemy. That cross bar is the one thing between them and success and a devilish little thing it is too, though hardly wider than their thumbs. Have you ever noticed the elation of a high jumper or a pole vaulter when he clears a height greater than he has done before? It is an interesting and a curious thing. It is almost as though he were saying, "There, blast you; I beat you that time." Have you ever noticed that when you are working with beginners, trying to teach them form, things go well if you have them working without the cross bar, but as soon as you set up the bar they become extremely conscious of it? So the coaching problem becomes, "How do you teach jumpers to beat the cross bar?"

DEVELOPING CONFIDENCE

Over-simplified, the answer is that you must give the boy confidence, belief in himself. The minute he loses that in a meet, he is through for the day. You must have noticed many times in meets the moment of doubt coming to the high jumper. He may have looked great clearing the previous height, but the instant that bar is raised one inch, he sees it as far more formidable. He may approach several times, revise his take-off mark, balk, and in other ways go to pieces. His next jump is often a pitiful effort, bearing no resemblance to the one with which he cleared that bar an inch lower. Confidence to any athlete is the super-extra, but to a high jumper it is a must. That cross bar is merciless and unyielding. It will not choke up like a human opponent.

THE IMPORTANCE OF THE APPROACH

To bring our jumpers to that point of confidence, we coaches have to start by eliminating some of the more common mistakes made by jumpers. We should begin by helping the boy gain confidence in his approach run. Nothing destroys a jumper's confidence faster than indecision about the run to the take-off. He needs to be sure of himself in that approach. The coach should insist first of all that the jumper establish a tentative take-off mark. It may be that you have decided upon a five-step approach. But the established take-off point and the number of steps to be used are only part of the preparation. Spend some time considering the boy's angle of approach. Too many coaches treat the angle of approach very casually and allow the jumper to take any angle that seems desirable to him. The truth is that the angle of approach plays a very important part in the bar clearance. Usually an approach angle of between 35 and 40 degrees will be suitable for most jumpers using the straddle or stomach roll

Figure 30

CARRUTHERS, U.S.A.—THE APPROACH TO THE HIGH JUMP.

Photo by Don Wilkinson

style, but you should be quick to notice that Valerie Brumel, the great Russian jumper, used a more acute angle of approach than most others. A few will be seen using a more nearly frontal approach. They are often jumpers who use some version of the dive roll. Technically, the angle approach from either left or right seems soundest. It allows the jumper more time to complete his rotation above the bar than does the frontal approach. You will be wise to experiment a little with your jumper to determine which angle of approach gives him best results. I believe that this matter of angle of approach deserves much more consideration than some coaches give it. It is my belief that it is quite individual and governed a great deal by the build of the athlete himself. See Figure 30.

Once the take-off mark, angle of approach and number of approach steps have been established tentatively, the coach may find some adjustments necessary. One of the factors that may force the adjustments is the speed of the approach run. This is often necessary because the athlete in his run back from the take-off mark to the mark indicating the start of his five-step approach or seven-step approach may be careless in the speed or length of stride he uses. As a result the marks are way off when he takes his real approach run. Usually the trouble arises because the jumper in running back to establish his marks will move too slowly. It is highly important that he make his run-back as consistent in speed and length of stride with his approach as possible. It means very little otherwise.

In building the confidence of his high jumper, the coach should hammer constantly at the consistency of the approach run. Some good high jump coaches that I have known can actually turn their backs on their jumper and tell you from the sound of his steps whether he is making a good approach or a poor one. It is because the approach run is so important to the jumper that I sympathize greatly with the athlete who finds himself forced by track conditions to run over obstacles such as the track curb or hedged in in such a way as to prevent his taking a full approach.

Figure 31a

CARRUTHERS, U.S.A., THE TAKE-OFF—PAN AM GAMES.

Figure 31b

BURRELL, U.S.A.—PAN AM GAMES.

This is definitely upsetting to a high jumper and should no more be allowed than incorrectly staggered starts in a race. Such conditions handicap some jumpers more than others. Fortunately, the new types of take-off areas have helped to eliminate the soft uneven surfaces found often in the past. Such things do shake the confidence of a high jumper, but they will shake him less if his coach has been adamant in his demands for consistent, rhythmic approach runs.

SOME THOUGHTS ABOUT TAKE-OFF

A study of the accompanying photographs showing jumpers at the point of take-off will illustrate slightly different styles, especially in the use of hands and arms (Figures 31a and 31b). The coach should be aware of the purposes in such arm movements and he should also be quick to notice certain features of the take-offs that are alike in all good high jumpers. He should note the hips, the position of the head, and the planting of the take-off foot. He should not overlook the use of the hands and arms at the take-off, considering carefully the differences between the style used by the Russian jumpers and that usually employed by the Americans.

A study of the take-off of Brumel and other Russian high jumpers reveals a forceful backward drive of both elbows and then the lift up over the take-off foot (Figures 32a, 32b and 32c). The coach should notice, however, that most of the best high jumpers in the United States, though they get a backward lean of the body as they go into the take-off, do not drive their elbows backward in the style of Brumel but reach high with the

129

Photo by Lou LaPrade,
Cape Cod Standard-Times

Photo by Joe Sherman

Figure 32a

Figure 32b

KENNY OF DENNIS YARMOUTH
HIGH SCHOOL—HIGH JUMP.

CARL GONZALVES—
MASSACHUSETTS STATE MEET.

inside arm turning slightly away from the cross bar. The Russians claim that their use of the arms is more efficient than the American style. Many of our coaches argue that the simple lift of the arms accomplishes the same things as the Russians seek without the added need of split-second timing in the sweep of the arms. If there is any advantage in the Russian style it would seem to me to be in the more vigorous upward thrust of the arms possible from the initial position of the elbows. Both styles emphasize the backward lean at take-off and the rock-up over the foot to get the drive of the whole foot into the spring. This is highly important since the length of time the foot remains in contact with the ground is going to have some effect upon the jump. The high jumper using his foot in the take-off is not unlike the sprinter driving against the starting blocks at the start of the dash. Both power and length of application of that power are involved in the take-off as they are in the sprinter's start.

If the coach wants to emphasize the type of point that will bring quick results and give the high jumper a little more confidence in himself, he should stress the high jumper's dropping his hips in the stride that precedes the planting of the foot for the take-off. This, one of the essential factors in good high jumping, is one that it is difficult to get a beginning jumper to recognize. Look at the loops or movies showing any of the best high jumpers in action and you will be quick to notice this definite dropping of the hips that helps the jumper gather for his take-off.

Most beginning jumpers have difficulty in mastering the backward lean and are inclined to do the opposite of what they should. They will turn the head and inside shoulder into the cross bar. In order to get his high jumper to get more vertical spring before his body rotation starts, the coach should have him working quite often on two-step jumping. If the bar is placed at a height several inches below the best that the jumper can do and he is sent at it in only a two-step approach, he will soon get the idea of getting as much height as possible before starting his rotation over the bar.

Figure 32c
CARL GONZALVES
CLEARING THE CROSS BAR

PREPARING FOR DIFFICULTIES

High jumpers seem easily upset over poor take-off areas and often perform poorly when they find a soft take-off or an approach that prevents their taking the usual number of steps. Because the soft take-off area is bothersome, it is wise to have the jumper work with a longer run in his approach. I have found that an added two steps in the approach run, if practiced often, can give the boy enough speed to offset the softness of the area. The added steps will also enable him to take off a little farther away from the cross bar and therefore in a spot that may not be so badly chewed up by other jumpers.

The coach can also assist his jumpers by having them do some practicing with shortened approach runs to prepare them for adverse conditions. He should realize that the psychological advantage is with his own high jumper when he is ready for unexpected situations which might be bothersome. If the coach knows that the jumping area in a field in which his jumping is to be done is restricted, he will be negligent if he does not spend some practice time that week having his high jumpers work under similar conditions.

CREATING TENSION IN OPPONENTS

Watching high jumpers in meets, I am often disturbed by the lack of concentration evident in the early jumps. I have seen many jumpers fail to clear at heights that were ridiculously low for them. In some scoring systems these early misses can be very costly because ties will not be allowed and the winner is established as the man with the fewest misses. But this is not the only loss to jumpers who become careless. The effect upon rival jumpers is important. Any high jumper gets to realize that he will have his "on" days and his "off" days. A jumper who may be

131

Figure 33a

CARRUTHERS, U.S.A.—PAN AM GAMES.

Figure 33b

BURRELL, U.S.A.—DURING MEN'S
HIGH JUMP, LOS ANGELES TIMES
INTERNATIONAL MEET.

worried about one of his opponents often gets a real psychological lift when his opponent misses early in the competition. It makes him feel that his opponent may be having an "off" day, and bolsters his confidence. See Figures 33a, 33b, 33c and 33d.

The coach should be urging his high jumpers to try to create the opposite impression on his rivals. He should stress the value of clearing on the first try and as decisively as possible. This can aid the jumper by making his rivals think that he is having an "on" day, thus adding to their worries. Such tactics as passing heights to conserve energy can be useful but the moment of truth must finally come, and it is on his first jump after passing heights that the jumper should try to clear the bar decisively. If he can do so after passing several heights, he will bother the more uncertain jumpers in the competition and perhaps get rid of them before the point scores are decided. I like to have my jumpers make every effort to clear the bar by wide margins on their early jumps. See Figures 34a and 34b.

Figure 33c

ERNIE SHELTON—BOTH ARMS ARE
SAFELY OUT OF THE WAY, THE HEAD,
SHOULDERS AND CHEST ARE CLEAR
AND SOMEWHAT LOWER THAN THE
HIPS, WHICH ARE ROLLING.

Figure 33d

BRUMEL, RUSSIA.

Photo by Don Wilkinson

Figure 34a

THE FAMOUS "FOSBURY FLIP"
DURING THE 1968 OLYMPICS.

Figure 34b

THE HIGH JUMP SEQUENCE.

Photos by Dr. Emil Dostal—Czech National Coach

High jumpers are frequently upset by little things that may escape the notice of the coach. For example, when the bar begins to get up there fairly high, some jumpers are bothered by having anyone who is quite short stand close to the uprights. The contrast between the short person and the height being attempted makes the jumper think that the bar is higher than it really is. Another thing that bothers the jumpers is having the cross bar either too short or set in such a way that it is not being used at its full length. Here again, the jumper gets the impression that the cross bar is higher than it actually is. The coach should be on the lookout for these little disturbing things and, whenever he can, see that they will not upset his own jumpers.

COACHING HELP FOR LONG JUMPERS

Because basic principles of dynamics indicate that speed is very important in long jumping, coaching has often been directed at improving the speed of the jumpers. What is often forgotten is that continuity of action is demanded and regardless of the speed of the approach run, the athlete's failure to keep his speed under control will nullify the speed that he uses. What must be kept in mind is that only as much speed as the jumper can control is of any value in the long jump, or for that matter, in any other event. I have seen a great deal of wasted speed in such events as the long jump, speed wasted because the athlete could not gather himself for the all-important lift off the take-off board. Instead, the long jumper almost literally ran off the board. This is one explanation of the difficulty that you may observe in some of your good sprinters when you try to make them into long jumpers. To be more exact in our demands, we should emphasize that *both* speed and control are necessary. If we could actually utilize the great speed of some of our world class sprinters in the long jump we would see some 30-foot long jumping. The truth is, however, that the full speed of such athletes cannot be used because it is practically impossible for the sprinter to use his top speed and still gather in the way that he must to get proper height at the take-off for effective long jumping. It is important that the coach realize that he must settle for something less than the athlete's top speed. Indeed, it is impossible for the sprinter to retain top speed and drop his hips in the last couple of steps before take-off as he must.

THE RELATIONSHIP OF SPEED TO LONG JUMPING

Naturally, some emphasis must be put upon the build-up of speed in the approach run, but it should never be stressed to the extent that the long jumper realizes his inability to get the lift he needs as he leaves the board. The coach should encourage his long jumper to use as long an approach run as he can to get to his best controlled speed. Some long jumpers are so bothered by their lack of control of their run that they settle for an approach that is too short to generate the speed that they need for effective jumping. The coach should work with his long jumpers to help them achieve evenness of stride. This will do a great deal to bolster the confidence of the jumper in his ability to hit the take-off board exactly. Though low hurdling is beginning to be dropped as an event in many areas, it has real value for teaching the long jumper how to combine good speed with evenness of stride. If you find your jumper bothered by unevenness in his strides in the approach run, you can help him greatly by having him running a series of low hurdles at regular low hurdle spacing. Some coaches like to use high hurdle practice for long jumpers. It is of some value, but since only three steps are used between high hurdles, the practice is not as effective as the speed work between low hurdles.

GETTING HEIGHT OFF THE BOARD

If your long jumper is having trouble getting height off the board, you can help him very much by having him concentrate upon shortening his last two strides and thus giving himself a chance to "gather" for his spring off the board. To insure his getting height in the jump, you should also emphasize that he keep the take-off leg slightly bent. This will help the jumper get the forward-upward spring that he wants. You should stress the point that his body weight should be slightly *ahead* of his take-off foot so that he will not get too much height and too little forward drive. With your beginning jumpers, you will find that most of your emphasis will have to be on getting the necessary lift off the board. Later you can make the slight adjustment to get the correct forward and upward motion. See Figure 35.

Figure 35
LONG JUMP SEQUENCE.

As you attempt to help your beginning jumpers, you should notice that when their weight is back of the take-off foot, their forward momentum is lessened. The most obvious example of this fault is seen when the long jumper has to reach for the board. The take-off leg is overextended and no lift results. Certainly this fault is a serious one, but since most long jumpers have trouble getting enough height in their jumps, I am reluctant to go along with the suggestion of some coaches that the long jumper should actually "run off the board." Young jumpers especially misunderstand such direction and fail miserably in getting height in their jumps. See Figure 36.

Figure 36

LYNN DAVIES, ENGLAND, UPSET THE CO-WORLD RECORD HOLDERS IN THE 1964 OLYMPIC BROAD JUMP FINAL.

Track and Field News

If you are concerned about the placement of the foot on the board at the take-off, I suggest that it is probably a *flat* placement. It seems to me that the speed of the jumper as a result of his approach run is too great to support any heel-ball-toe action. In fact the speed of the approach run allows very little time for foot contact with the board. This is another factor in the limitation of speed that can be used in the long jump. The faster the runner is coming, the less time his take-off foot has contact with the take-off board. Here again is that principle involved in the force applied and the length of time of its application.

In your efforts to assist your long jumpers, you should not overlook the necessity of their getting full stretch of the take-off leg to get the range of action for a good pull through for the step action in air. Watch your jumper's head to see that he has really lifted it at the time of take-off. His eyes should be up and his chest held high as long as possible (Figure 37).

Figure 37

RALPH BOSTON, U.S.A.—DURING MEN'S LONG JUMP AT LOS ANGELES
TIMES INTERNATIONAL MEET.

See that the knee of the take-off leg is driven high and that the free leg stretches down, then goes forward and down and straight under the jumper's body. The take-off leg is pulled through *bent*. The free leg should bend up behind. As the jumper is about to land, his heels should be forced forward side by side ahead of the body. Insist that the arms be held high and that they move in a sprint action. There seems to be merit in the insistence of some coaches that the thigh of neither leg should go farther back than the line from the head to the ground.

THE IMPORTANCE OF THE LANDING

Considering the fact that many long jumps are won by inches, there seems to be too little attention given to the long jumper's landing. To get the most out of the jump, the athlete should stretch his legs ahead as far as possible, holding them together and swinging his arms backward as he drops his head between his knees and moves his body over his feet as he hits the pit. Remember that the jumper who falls to the side has not made a full effort. Usually he has not had enough height at the take-off.

Some attention should be given to wild arm action in the jump. Above all the coach should realize that starting the hitch kick too soon will spoil the jump. He should also be aware that dropping the trunk upon the thighs prematurely in the landing action will force the jumper's legs down too soon.

Finally, to prevent the fretting of the jumper about wind conditions and poor surface of runways, the coach should emphasize that the changing of check marks should be expected and that the jumper should recognize such factors and compensate for them. By preparing his jumpers for such problems, the coach can give them a psychological advantage over those opponents who let themselves be upset by adverse conditions.

Chapter 7 | COACHING THE FIBRE GLASS POLE VAULTER

FROM THE TIME THAT THE FIBRE GLASS POLE REVOLU-
tionized this event, the coach has been faced with a real motivational
problem. Even the bamboo and the metal poles made this event difficult
enough to coach. The bamboo pole, now forgotten in most countries, presented its own problem. If you have been coaching long enough to remember the sight of the pole splintering beneath the vaulter as he pushed on it
while high in the air, you know how difficult it was to get him over the
fear of the pole itself. The metal pole, aluminum or steel, gave the vaulter
confidence (Figure 38). He had the feeling that he could rely on the pole
to support him while he did his gymnastics in the air. He no longer had
to fear the long, dagger-like spikes that threatened him when the bamboo
pole splintered under him as he tried to push up from it.

If you were coaching in the days of the bamboo pole you will recall
the necessity of making the vaulter return to the vault immediately after
he had felt a pole collapse beneath him. You knew how important it was
to help him to regain some of his confidence in the pole. If you gave him
too much time to think about what had just happened to him, you realized
that he might "psyche" himself right out of the event. Strangely enough,
the coach today is faced with a somewhat similar problem in the pole
vault. It is very difficult to instill confidence in the vaulter that his fibre
glass pole will support him and will release the energy that he has stored
in it as he rocks back and waits, suspended above the runway. In this
respect at least, we are back to the problem presented by the bamboo pole.
Even the best of our vaulters will admit to you the feeling of uncertainty
that they have as they feel the glass pole bend beneath their weight and
wonder whether it is going to do its job. The coach who tries to laugh off

Figure 38
LORING DAY SEQUENCE.

the fear of his young vaulters is not being realistic. It takes real nerve to rock back on a glass pole and drive your legs skyward, trusting it to do its work. If your vaulter has ever had a pole break on him or release in

Figure 39
BRIAN STERNBERG VAULTING.

140

an unexpected way so that he has been thrown to the side and landed close to the edge of the landing pit, you can be sure that both of you have a real problem to face. Such an experience can shatter the confidence of a beginning vaulter so much that he may never trust the pole again. Fibre glass poles do break quite often, and most beginning vaulters know this. See Figure 39.

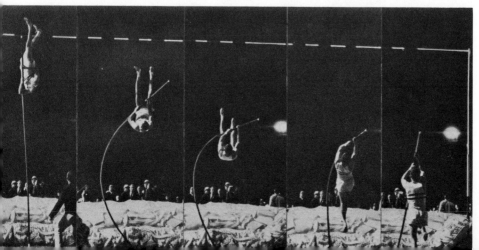

CORRECTING FALLACIES

It is quite a temptation to the coach to have his beginning vaulters start with a fibre glass pole that they can bend. He knows the story of the stored energy in the bent pole that can flip his vaulter skyward. But for two important reasons, he should *not* start his athletes with a pole that they can bend with little effort. First of all, the vaulter who is learning to use the fibre glass pole is going to be bothered by the extreme flexibility of the pole and be concerned about trusting himself to it. Secondly, the fact is that the pole that bends too easily is not storing energy that will be returned to lift him over the bar. Like an elastic band that can be stretched without effort or a bow that can be bent very easily, the fibre glass pole that can be bent almost effortlessly snaps back with very little force. The good vaulters know that they must exert real effort to get that bend in the pole that they need. The speed of the approach and the drive into the take-off box are the big factors in getting useful bend in the pole. If you have your beginning vaulters using poles that are suited for lighter athletes, you are creating problems for yourself and for them.

CREATING CONFIDENCE FOR THE WAIT

If you have been working with vaulters who use the fibre glass pole, you must have encountered the big problem with such vaulters many times. You know how difficult it is to get your vaulter to rock back and wait for the pole to do its work (Figure 40). Here again you are faced with the

Scholastic Coach Photo

Figure 40

KEN WELLS OF HENRY GUNN HIGH SETTING A NEW NORTH COAST SECTION CLASS "B" RECORD AT 13½ FEET IN SANTA ROSA, CALIFORNIA.

necessity of creating confidence in your vaulter. Somehow you must make him have enough faith in his pole to trust it while he lies there on his back high above the runway, his feet lifted above his head and an unspoken prayer on his lips that the pole will unbend and not break before it flips him up and over the cross bar. You had better believe that it is far easier for you to urge your vaulter to lie back and wait for the pole to release its energy than it is for him to do it. If you have been working with a vaulter who has previously used a metal pole, you should realize that the very bend of the fibre glass pole which makes it better than the metal one is what creates the problem. It seems to me that the most sensible approach to this problem is to tell your vaulter frankly that you realize how easy it is for you to tell him to trust the pole but how difficult it is for him to do it. You have to convince him that there is no easy way out. Until he has enough confidence to lie back, holding his body away from the pole until it releases its energy, he will gain very little from the fibre glass pole (Figure 41). Perhaps the most valuable motivation you can offer will be the result of the athlete's belief in you. Here is a real test of your coaching worth. If your vaulter does not have faith in his pole, he must have faith in you and your advice.

NOTICING THE DIRECTION OF POLE BEND

Another point that most of today's vaulters seem to neglect is that of noticing carefully in what direction the glass pole bends. A good coach will insist that his vaulter pay close attention to the action of his pole, noticing whether it bends to the left, as most poles do, or somewhat back-

Figure 41

J. PENNEL ATTEMPTING 17-9¼ AT LOS ANGELES TIMES INTERNATIONAL MEET.

Photo by Don Wilkinson

ward. His knowledge of how the pole bends should have an important effect upon his timing of his leg lift and pull up on the pole.

The action involved in fibre glass pole vaulting is sometimes described as a "compound pendulum." The vaulter is actually swinging around his hands while the pole is swinging around a center of rotation, the take-off box. This description, to a certain point, is accurate, but it seems to me that the vaulter will get a more accurate picture of what is happening if he thinks of himself as swinging around a pole which is moving more like the arm of a metronome; it is moving certainly, not quite like a pendulum suspended from above, as he himself is, but rather moving from a point *below*.

The boy must be made to realize that the pole *has no energy at all until he stores it* by means of his run and take-off. *At the right time* he then withdraws that energy that he has stored in the pole.

If the vaulter hangs low on the pole, it will move rapidly toward the crossbar. If he pulls up too quickly, the forward motion of the pole will stop.

Perhaps the most difficult point to bring home to the vaulter is the fact that when the pole bends, the vaulter's center of gravity *rises very slowly* while the vaulter moves toward the cross bar rapidly. The vaulter must compensate by rocking backward away from the bar *very fast*. If the vaulter does this correctly, *he gains time*. According to actual studies, he has about one-quarter of a second in which to act. He must lift his legs vertically along the axis of the pole as he rocks back. In this manner, he keeps his center of gravity back under his hand grip. The vaulter must control the pole speed toward the cross bar and the lift of the body according to the forward speed of the pole. If the vaulter allows his center of gravity to get in front of the pole, the pole drives him forward too fast. He must concentrate on vertical drive while the pole straightens.

THE ROCK BACK

The sinking sensation as the pole bends is rather frightening to the beginning vaulter, but it is this fear that you must help him overcome. He *must* rock back and get his hips above his hands. Dick Ganslen in his great study of the mechanics of pole vaulting points out that the higher the vaulter goes, the more time he has to elevate his legs. It is the vaulter who is struggling over 10 or 11 feet who has very little time to complete the vaulting action. The Perrin Vault Trainer is a device that is very valuable in preparing the beginner for the sensation that he encounters while waiting for the bent pole to release.

If you had the opportunity of watching the vaulters in the Mexico

Olympics, you must have noticed how vaulters are beginning to use longer approach runs to build up speed for greater storage of energy in the pole. I feel that any good vaulter should be encouraged to experiment with a little longer run. Some use very short approach runs, hardly more than 90 feet. When we consider the fact that sprinters need about 50 yards to reach top speed, we can see the possible advantage of using runs of from 120 to 150 feet in the pole vault approach.

The coach will need to watch his vaulter very closely as he adds speed to his approach. He must remember that the vaulter must now concentrate more than ever on the rock-back. If the vaulter using greater speed lets his body get past the pole too soon, it will drive him forward more rapidly into the cross bar. The coach must make the vaulter realize that the more speed he uses in his approach and the greater his drive into the take-off box, the more he must rock back and the longer he must wait for the pole to release its energy.

WIND CONDITIONS RELATING TO THE APPROACH

In coaching your pole vaulters, you should not overlook the effects of the wind upon his approach. If the wind is directly in his face, he will have to change his marks, moving them in so that he can get into good take-off position. Under such wind conditions, his tendency will be to come short of his mark and have to reach to get into take-off position. With the glass pole, this can be a fatal mistake because the vaulter must drive into the box with all possible speed to get the full benefit of the take-off.

What has been pointed out about the problems that result from running into the wind is just as important in the vaulter's reaction to differences in runways. The fast runway must be considered very much like the approach with the wind at the vaulter's back. He may find himself overrunning his take-off mark. This means that he must move his marks back. You will be giving him good coaching advice if you remind him that he must adjust his run to offset either wind direction or runway speed.

PLACING THE UPRIGHTS

Still another factor in your vaulter's success or failure is the placement of the uprights. You should know the rights that the rules guarantee your vaulter. When you observe that your vaulter is hitting the cross bar on his way up, you should insist that he demand that the uprights be moved backward toward the pit as far as the rules allow. He will then have more time in which to lift his legs before they reach the cross bar. On the other hand, if your vaulter is coming down on the bar, you must insist that he have the uprights moved closer to the take-off box so that he can get his greatest height above the bar.

Another important consideration in vaulting with the glass pole is that of the athlete's use of his head in the rock back. For quite a while early in the day of the glass pole there was a theory that the vaulter in his rock back should deliberately drop his head backward to assist him in staying away from the pole in this stage of the vault. More careful analysis has led to the advice to hold the head steady and *not* to drop it backward. Furthermore, with beginning vaulters and even occasionally with experienced vaulters, the old method of dropping the head backward led to trouble. The vaulter who had not mastered control of the bend found that he was being flipped upward or forward in such a manner that he received a severe snap of the neck and sometimes some rather painful effects. For the coach trying to instill enough confidence in his vaulter to rock back and wait for the bend and release of the pole this effect caused an added problem. He found that the vaulter recalled the unpleasant sensation of the snap of the neck and became more reluctant to rock back. The idea of the deliberate drop back of the head is still being taught in some areas where coaches have not learned of the newest findings. This is just one more example of how much there is still to be learned about vaulting with the glass pole.

THE MATCHING OF POLE AND VAULTER

One of the best things that has happened in fibre glass pole vaulting has been the recent study by the manufacturers to improve the poles themselves. Their attention to improvement of the texture of the material has helped to lessen the danger of breaking poles. Aside from the expense involved in the high mortality of glass poles during the early stages of their use, there was the mental and sometimes physical damage done. It will be wise for the coach to give serious attention to the weight of his vaulter and the glass pole advised for his use. Some coaches have been over-eager to find a pole that the boy can bend easily, and have had him working with a pole intended for someone of lighter weight. As has already been mentioned in this chapter the pole that bends easily is not the answer to better vaulting, and of even more importance it can be downright dangerous for the boy using it. One experience with the pole breaking beneath him while he is in air and the resulting toss in an unpredictable direction can set the boy back so far that the coach has his whole job to do over.

WEIGHT TRAINING IS VALUABLE

With the fibre glass pole, certain aspects of vaulting become easier, but others make new demands upon the body. The need to rock back and yet lift the legs high above the head to await the snap of the pole makes abdominal strength more important than ever in pole vaulting. Always important, though often neglected, in pole vaulting, abdominal strength now becomes more essential. Of all weight exercises used with the vaulter, sit-ups with weights of gradually increasing poundage are, in my opinion, of the greatest value. Weight training to strengthen the upper body is still very important as are leg strength exercises. Any observant coach should note the increasing effort of good vaulters to sprint at full speed into the pole plant and to take off with top hand actually behind the head. This is a demand upon arm and shoulder strength. Weight training and flexibility exercises should be recommended to the vaulter for such strength development.

The hand hold with the glass pole differs widely from that used with the old metal poles. The wide spread between the hands varies somewhat among the top vaulters. The coach should realize that many beginning vaulters are having problems because they are still trying to slide their bottom hand up the pole at take-off as was done with the metal pole. Sometimes this is the basis of their difficulty in getting the glass pole to bend. The vaulter who had difficulty sliding the hand up the metal pole now has one less difficulty to worry about. He can set his hands and keep them spread. I have a feeling, however, that we will see future progress in this aspect of fibre glass pole vaulting. Already some are experimenting with closer hand holds, and as poles themselves are improved I think that we will see efforts made to slide the hands together as vaulters used to do with the metal poles. Mastery of the bend without the wide hand spread may lead to this development.

Though some glass pole users are employing the jackknife type of clearance, you will notice that a great deal of attention is being given to the flyaway style. Many vaulters in their efforts to get maximum height with their legs as they await the release of the pole's energy are driving their feet almost straight above their heads as they push off the pole. They are relying on the snap of the pole to drive them upward and at the same time forward enough to clear the bar. These vaulters are using every effort to keep their legs high as long as possible, and they feel that dropping the legs in the jackknife position demands delicate timing if they are to get maximum lift from the pole (Figures 42 and 43). The margin for error is very slight.

Whether you are a high school coach trying to get your beginner to clear ten feet or a coach of world class athletes trying to help your vaulter to a new world's record, you need to keep this in mind. At the time of this writing, there is no pole made that can stand the highest hand hold possible for the vaulter combined with the best and most uniform bend of

Photo by Don Wilkinson

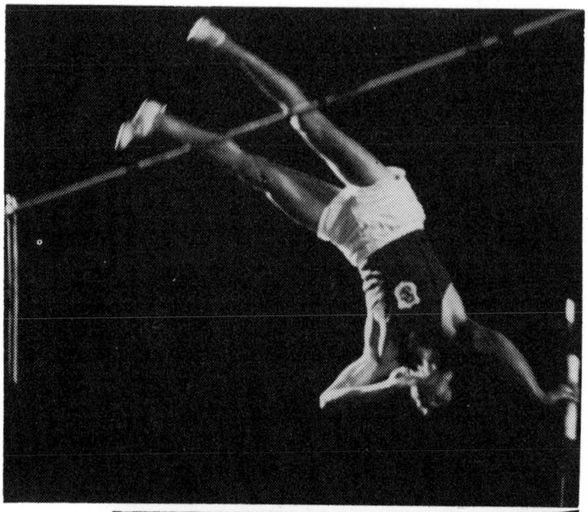

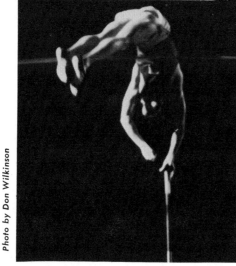

Figure 42
SEAGREN CLEARING 17-4 AT THE NCAA MEET, PROVO, UTAH.

Photo by Don Wilkinson

Figure 43
PAUL WILSON CLEARING 17-4 AT NCAA MEET, PROVO, UTAH.

the pole. This means that the vaulter who wants to use the highest handhold possible for him and still get the maximum bend of the pole cannot use the pole suited to his weight. He must settle for the pole recommended for the next weight class. I am sure that before long pole manufacturers will find the solution to this problem and come up with a pole that will allow for approach speed, weight of the vaulter, and maximum bend with its resulting storage of energy in the pole. For the time being, however, the coach will do well to advise his vaulters to work with a pole geared to a weight slightly above their own. The pleasantest thing that I can say here is that I see many indications that pole manufacturers are turning to some of our leading experts on pole vaulting to find some of the answers to better pole construction.

Too few of our United States coaches realize how much has been done to make their job easier. Our vaulters and jumpers no longer can blame hard landing pits for their reluctance to do what is necessary for good performances. Portable pits and an abundance of sponge rubber to cushion the landing shock have been a great help to all of us in our attempts to get our jumpers and vaulters to perform without fear of injury. You have only to visit other countries of the world to realize how fortunate we are here. Any coach is remiss in his motivation if he fails to remind his pole vaulters that they need have no fear of landing in the shock absorbent areas we have today.

To conclude this chapter on fibre glass pole vaulting, I want to make a few observations and recommendations which are mine alone and that I may later regret. I cannot point to test results or mechanics of athletics to prove my points. I merely suggest that coaches give some thought to my ideas and that some of them may prove worthwhile.

First, let me urge the coach to stress the importance of trying to clear the bar convincingly on the first effort each time. Already some of our rules are based upon the fewest misses as well as the height cleared. In the future, this method of determining winners may become more and more necessary.

Next, may I suggest that there should be more and more emphasis upon the timing of the pull-up and push-off in glass pole vaulting. I am convinced that the vaulter who gets his legs high in the air when the pole begins to straighten must not only drive his legs up parallel to the pole but must also raise his pelvis and *stretch* upward to complete the swing-up on the pole. It seems to me that the greater the height the vaulter attempts, the more important this lift of the pelvis and straightening of the hips become.

Still another feeling of mine is that most vaulters are timing their pull-up and the start of their turn rather casually. I think that both the pull-up and the turn are usually started too soon. It may well be that as vaulters get used to the action of the glass pole, they will begin to refine these phases of the vault. In my opinion, most vaulters release the pole too soon. Some of the best efforts have been those for which we have pictorial evidence that the vaulter stayed with his pole until it had fully straightened.

WORKING WITH THE
Chapter | PROSPECTIVE
8 | RECORD BREAKER

$\mathbf{M}$OST INTERESTING, YET MOST FRUSTRATING AT TIMES, is the experience of working with a prospective record breaker. For some strange reason, it seems to make little difference whether the athlete is threatening merely a high school state record or an intercollegiate mark of long standing. In either instance, the athlete stands out among his fellows. He soon realizes that he is being watched and judged. He finds that his team-mates, his coach, and even his opponents seem to be expecting outstanding performances from him. This combination of admiration and expectation can be a source of inspiration to the athlete and lead him to brilliant performances, or it can be a source of great pressure and force him into very disappointing efforts. It seems to me that nothing in track and field requires more careful *individual* attention than the coaching of the young man who stands out above his mates and is a real threat to any record whether it be dash or distance, discus throw or decathlon. Most of us who have coached for a long time have seen boys who rose to the challenge and others who collapsed under the pressure. Many coaches who envy those who are blessed with athletes who threaten the records find themselves more disturbed than happy when they find such young men in their squads.

THE IMPORTANCE OF INDIVIDUAL ATTENTION

Though it is true that some of our finest athletes are our most coach-able ones, we coaches find that it really isn't easy to be at the top. Perhaps one reason why we find the experience a trying one is that it forces us to stop thinking in general terms and begin thinking in specifics. We have to start planning workouts to match the talents of the boy who finds the train-

150

ing schedule for the average athlete no real challenge. He is physically the equivalent of the gifted classroom student who finds the ordinary class routine too dull. The outstanding athlete like the outstanding scholar forces his teacher to consider him individually. Unfortunately, the very needs of such an athlete may lead to another problem for the coach. When he does begin to pay special attention to his star, he is likely to find the other members of his squad murmuring about his being interested only in the top man. The coach had better steel himself against such criticism, because he is encountering admiration mixed with envy. The boys with limited talent really admire their outstanding teammate, but they just as surely envy him. Their grumbling cannot be ignored if the coach is interested in team effort. On the other hand, neither can the star be given the same treatment as the mediocre athlete. To be brutally honest about the matter, I consider this one of the stiffest tests that a coach can face.

THE STAR AS A TEAM AID

Let's assume that your star happens to be a hurdler. He may be so far superior to your other hurdle prospects that there is more contrast than comparison. When some of my former stars read this they will probably realize what I was trying to do with them and to them. For that I offer no apologies. I am sure that if it works for you, you will feel that you have done your best for both your star and your weakling. I found that I could give my star special attention without causing resentment if I made him work with the less gifted athletes in his event to help them improve their form. I frequently went over with the star the points that I wanted him to emphasize. I found that this device seemed to make the lesser athletes lose some of their resentment toward him. And you had better believe that it was there, or you just don't know human nature. What the star did not know was that I was often forcing him to study more closely his own weak points as he tried to correct them in others. Perhaps you will sense, as I sometimes did, that your average athletes begin to have a disquieting tendency to turn to your star for help with their problems rather than to you. You can salvage some of your pride if you remember that you were the one who made your star forget himself long enough to help those less gifted than himself.

USING THE STATUS SYMBOL

Whether the prospective record breaker you are working with is a sprinter or a shot putter, a miler or a discus thrower, you are faced with the same problem. What you must really try to do is to make the athlete conscious that he has the potential of being a *status symbol*. You are really trying to convince him that the all-out effort necessary to make him a record breaker is what will set him apart and above his fellow athletes. For a time at least, he will be able to say to himself, "I am the best!" This is true whether it means *best* in his league, in his state, in his country or in the world. Fortunately there seems to be in all of us, great or small, a yearning to be the best. For some it will always be no more than a dream, but for others it can be a driving influence that is truly amazing. Whether your prospective record breaker will make the grade or not is usually determined by the amount of dedication you find associated with his talent. See Figure 44.

Photo by Don Wilkinson

Figure 44

FOUR WORLD'S RECORD HOLDERS—MATSON, SEAGREN, GREENE, SMITH.

Both coach and athlete need to realize that talent in itself is not much to be proud of; it is God-given. What the athlete does with that talent that he possesses is what lifts him above the average. To me it is more heartbreaking to see a talented athlete satisfied with efforts far below his potential, than to see an untalented one driving himself hopelessly.

In their fine book, *Problem Athletes and How to Handle Them,* Dr. Bruce Ogilvie and Dr. Thomas Tutko have made some interesting observations about the prospective record breaker. They contend that their tests have shown that it takes a special kind of person, psychologically, to set a record. Speaking in terms of a world's record, they point out that he must go beyond all those who have previously attempted the event. They add, "He must have that inner quality which says, 'It is a good thing to break this standard.' "

THE SIGNIFICANCE OF "INNER DRIVE"

I would even expand upon their contention and suggest to you as a coach that, relatively speaking, the same thing is true whether the athlete is merely trying for a league record or a meet record. In a limited sense he faces the same problem. He is trying to do something that no man in his league has ever accomplished or that any competitor in this meet has ever achieved. His sights may be set upon a 60-foot record with the 12-pound shot or upon a sub-two minute half mile rather than a world record in his event, but his problem is the same.

Occasionally in your dealings with track athletes you are bound to come upon one who wants more than anything else to break a record. Such athletes are likely to be willing to punish themselves in practice far beyond the average. If such an athlete has talent, you can be sure that he is a potential record breaker in his event. It will take some mighty poor coaching to stop him. On the other hand, if he lacks the necessary talent for his event, you will accomplish more by steering him into an event more suited to his goal. He will never be satisfied in the event which balks him in his efforts to be a record breaker. At times the athlete with limited talents but high aspirations can accomplish surprising things, but frequently he can be a rather tragic figure.

PLANNING THE ATTACKS OF THE RECORD

If you find yourself with an athlete who shows this great desire to be the best, you can help him in several ways. Many coaches will suggest that you point the athlete for one great, all-out effort. I feel differently about it. I am thinking about the many obstacles beyond the control of the athlete and his coach that can arise when everything hinges upon that one great effort. Weather, track conditions, lack of competition, and other factors can thwart the athlete who points for one major strike. I think also of the after-effects of an attempt that fails and the possible reaction of the athlete.

Considering all these things, I feel that the coach is wise to plan for more than one assault on the record. Perhaps he can set three dates not too far apart on which the athlete is to make a determined effort to set the record. Under certain circumstances, of course, this may not be possible. Some leagues recognize records set in regular league competition, but others accept only those set in their championship meets. Under the latter rule, the prospective record breaker must set his sights upon that one big effort if he is to get the recognition he seeks. Yet even when such rules hold, I like to plan more than one strike at the record. I will encourage the athlete to make a great effort in a preliminary meet with the purpose of building up his confidence if he succeeds in bettering the record time or distance. If he fails, he still has time to work on the things that spoiled his effort so the blow will not be a final one.

CHECKING AND USING THE OPPOSITION

Although in many attempts to break records in such running events as the distance races it is necessary for the prospective record breaker to set his own pace, this is not always so. Very often an athlete can be assisted in his record-breaking attempt by studying and using his opponents. For example, if he is taking a crack at a mile record in his league, he should be helped by his coach's study of the opposition. If the coach is aware of opponents who like to move out fast in the opening quarter of the mile, he can have his star use them as pace makers in the early part of the race. He will thus be able to avoid settling into a slow pace which may endanger his effort to set the new record. On the other hand, if the coach knows that his man's opponents like to ease the pace in the early stages of the race, he can insist upon his boy's moving to the front immediately or he can have one of his own runners go to the front to set the pace necessary to assure the record.

PLAYING UP THE ATHLETE'S STRENGTHS

In the track events, the coach should always take full advantage of his athlete's strong points. If the boy is to have his best chance at setting a record, it is a serious mistake not to make use of his early speed. An attempt to save it for the final stages of the race can backfire. The boy is really racing the stopwatch so it is a mistake to lose time to it while he is fresh. If he drives himself during the major part of his race, the prospective record breaker is going to find the reserve strength he needs in the final stages because he will see the record within his reach. More track men lose their bids for records through holding too much in reserve than by running themselves out too early.

TENSION AND THE OUTSTANDING ATHLETE

Far more rarely than one might expect does the outstanding athlete find everything going for him. If he feels in top shape, he often finds weather conditions troublesome. If he feels ready for a top effort he may find that he has drawn a poor starting position in a race or that the field opposing him is so large that he must suffer through long delays while he awaits his turn to jump or throw. He may be cut off as he goes to make his big move in a race, or he may find that his approach run is restricted in the jumps or the pole vault. He may face the annoyance of a poor putting or throwing surface. This is something that the prospective record breaker must accept; he cannot wait for the time when everything is ideal. That time comes perhaps once in a lifetime. If conditions are bad, the athlete must either make his bid in the face of them or forget his attempt at the record on that day.

A very great pole vaulter told me once that the only thing he considered was his own feeling. He said, "If I feel that I am right, that's when I go for broke. I don't worry about petty annoyances. I figure that my self confidence is going to more than offset such things as supposedly slow runways."

One of America's greatest milers once told me, "I never walk up to start a race against even the weakest opponents without feeling butterflies in my stomach. If I let something like that stop me, I would never have set a record."

These men were U.S. Olympic stars, so your prospective record breaker must realize that if such men admit the rarity of ideal conditions and even of the never-ceasing feeling of fear at the start of an event, he can hardly expect to be any different. If he is ready, that little knot at the pit of his stomach will disappear as he goes into action, and the trivial annoyances will be forgotten in the intensity of his effort.

CONSIDERATIONS FOR THE FUTURE

As records get better and better, I feel sure that track and field rules will be changed to permit certain practices now frowned upon. The day is not so distant when starting blocks were not allowed in the sprints. Even more recently the rules for the high jump were altered to allow the many styles of high jumping that we now see, including the "Fosbury Flip." The extra distance allowed to the baton receiver in a sprint relay to build up speed ahead of the passing zone resulted from an even more recent rule change. Implements themselves have undergone great changes and great improvements. Consider the great difference from the bamboo to the fibre glass pole. Little by little we are going to see rules changed to open the way to new styles in various events and new implements devised to shatter existing records.

Have you ever stopped to ask yourself why shot putters and hammer throwers must compete from the restrictions of a seven-foot circle while discus throwers are allowed a larger one? Have you ever wondered why javelin throwers, long jumpers, pole vaulters, high jumpers, and triple jumpers may use as long a run as they wish to build up speed for their effort, yet discus throwers, hammer throwers, and shot putters must compete from sharply restricted areas? Traditional though these restrictions are, they are being whittled away bit by bit. Do not be too surprised if within your lifetime such rules are changed. The wide take-off board now permitted in high school competition may soon be accepted for all levels of competition.

As fractions of seconds become more and more important in distance races, there is bound to be recognition of the importance of those saved at the *beginning* of the race. It may not be long before we see milers and two milers using starting blocks. And *why not?* If they are recognized as a definite aid to the sprinter, why should they not be used by the distance runner? The prospective record breaker of the future may find his task so demanding that any device that can save him a fraction of a second or give him an added foot of distance will be put to use.

Part II
Team Motivation

	PREPARATION
Chapter	FOR ADVERSE
9	CONDITIONS

You SHOULD NOTE FIRST OF ALL THAT I HAVE ENTITLED this chapter "Preparation *For* Adverse Conditions," not "Preparation *Under* Adverse Conditions." No matter what section of the country you coach in, you can point to difficulties that affect your training plans for the athletes on your teams. It may be that the frigid winters and cold wet springs of New England restrict your outdoor workouts. But the marathoners and such distance stars as Jim Ryun himself mock at the weather as they train over snow covered roads or bundle up in sweat suits and gloves and hats to get their miles of training done. Perhaps the muggy, hot days in the South and Southwest challenge your athletes. But they merely offer discomfort that many of our country's best athletes have learned to endure. Low humid coastal plains or high mountain areas with their rarefied air present conditions which athletes accustomed to train in them learn to overcome. But what I am discussing in this chapter is not the training of athletes who are accustomed to these conditions; it is rather the training of athletes to whom these difficulties, under which they must compete, are unfamiliar.

THE VALUE OF MODERN INVESTIGATIONS

Perhaps never before in our many years of track and field has there been such concern about and study of adverse conditions as there was during the preparations for the 1968 Olympics in Mexico City. Nations from

159

all corners of the earth whose athletes were eyeing the greatest goal in all track and field, an Olympic gold medal, sent teams of experts to check the effects of high altitude on athletic performance. You will do well to observe that their studies were not restricted to the long distance runs. They delved much deeper and considered the possible effects on many different types of athletes, ranging all the way from sprinters to swimmers. I have read the reports turned in by the medical teams of several nations and talked with some of the leading authorities belonging to such teams. From your newspapers, many of you may have learned about the deep concern of most of them about the effects upon long distance runners. Some were more outspoken than others in their insistence that adequate preparation at high altitudes be provided for those who must compete in the long distance runs at such high altitude. Others called attention to threats of another nature. Stomach ailments that beset the tourists in Mexico City were stressed as threats to good performances by athletes. Their studies turned up some mighty interesting evidence to justify their concern about the calibre of performances under similar or nearly similar conditions. As a result of the reports turned in by their teams of experts, some nations have been quite frank in their criticism of such places as Mexico City as sites for Olympic competition. Results in the 1968 Olympics seem to have proved their fears well justified.

Now your reaction to all of this may be, "What's that to me? I'm not preparing a man for the Olympics. I'm worried about the teams on my schedule that I must meet regularly." However, Coach, If you are looking forward to another ten or fifteen years of working with track and field teams in any part of this country or any other, you are going to have to consider some of the findings of these carefully selected groups of experts. It seems to me that one of the areas that coaches have neglected most is that of preparing athletes for competition under adverse conditions. The impact of such necessity will be greater as air travel makes regional and even national competition much easier.

But even if you feel that the teams you coach will not be involved in intersectional competition now or ten years from now, you should not toss aside lightly the findings and subsequent recommendations of the teams of medical experts who have made studies and used tests to supply definite scientific evidence to justify their claims. If you don't want to be left behind in this business of coaching track and field, you should recognize the contributions that scientific study has made to the improvement of performance in almost every event. If you can read a book such as Geoffrey Dyson's *The Mechanics of Athletics* and still argue that you can coach as well with hit-or-miss theories, you are a rare individual and perhaps a bit luckier than most of us. If you can see all of the evidence indicating that weight training geared to specific events has contributed greatly to outstanding performances and still hold to the old theory that weight lifting is restrictive and muscle binding, you are deceiving yourself. Hardly an event in track or field has not been aided by scientific study and testing. I firmly believe that the future will make coaching by guess work as outmoded as vaulting with bamboo poles.

It seems to me that these teams of medical and psychological experts have done much more than bring out the problems involved in high altitude racing for distance men. They have focused our attention on related influences that affect the coaching of athletes under conditions not usually thought of as especially significant. Like Mark Twain, we often complain about the weather and though we know that we can do nothing to change it, we seldom do much to prepare for competition under the conditions that we moan about.

We may argue that we in the East rarely have to worry about excessive heat and humidity during our racing seasons, but we overlook the fact that we frequently find our state championship meets in early June contested in extremely hot weather as the sun beats down mercilessly during the day-long meets. I have sat for hours under a boiling sun too many dozens of times to swallow the suggestion that meets will be contested on pleasant, stimulating days. Yet I have observed that many coaches who get a siege of hot, humid weather a week or two ahead of their state championship meets, are likely to ease up on their athletes, offering the stifling weather as an excuse. It seems to me that such coaches are overlooking a real opportunity. They know that such spells of weather may persist for days and days; yet they do very little to prepare their teams for the very type of weather under which they may have to compete. I consider this a mistake.

ORDINARY PRECAUTIONS ARE NOT ENOUGH

Don't make the mistake of thinking that I am advocating a "practice as usual" procedure. No coach in his right mind would contend that times on a cold, windy day are the same as those run on a hot, humid day. What the body must do to meet the stresses of extreme cold or heat can limit the performance it can give under such conditions. Athletes, whether of high school age or of college age, can be mighty foolish about meeting unexpected extremes in weather conditions. Oh, most coaches will warn their athletes to relax in shady spots on very hot days, or remind them to keep on their sweat suits and warm up well on cold, blustery days. These are elementary things that most athletes will have sense enough to do without being reminded. It is preparation beyond such ordinary precautions that I want to suggest here.

SOME THOUGHTS ABOUT VARYING APPROACHES

There can often be a tremendous psychological impact upon an athlete who runs into unexpected extremes in the weather on the day when he hoped to be able to perform at his best. Some will be more seriously upset than others. It is for this reason that I think that the wise coach will seize the opportunity to have his athletes work out under unusually difficult weather conditions. Both the coach and the athlete need to find out what effects such difficulties will have upon performances.

The discus thrower who has practiced throwing into a head wind as well as with a following wind will know something about the effects of each upon his discus flight. The javelin thrower who has practiced throwing into a left to right cross wind will realize what it can do to the javelin whose point falls off to the right as he delivers it. Nothing can teach him the weakness of such a throw better than learning the way in which a left to right cross wind can exaggerate the failure to bring the javelin through in a long pull straight over the shoulder.

A long jumper who has checked his approach run only when the wind is at his back cannot appreciate the big difference in his stride against a strong wind in his face. If the coach has done a thorough job, he will have his jumper prepare two sets of check marks, one taken with a following run and another with a strong wind against him. If the athlete does this, he has an immediate psychological advantage over the one who comes poorly prepared. I have seen quite a few examples of good jumpers being badly upset by unexpected wind conditions and performing far below their capabilities.

Though some coaches might question the wisdom of such tactics, I have on some occasions had my high jumpers practice with both five- and seven-stride approaches so that they would be ready for good performances even if they found the high jump approaches allowing a shorter run than expected. I feel that the coach is unwise to overlook the very frequent restrictions on high jump approach runs found among tracks, especially in high school competition.

PRACTICING IN THE RAIN

Though many high school and college athletes have learned to practice their events in the rain, there are still many who find a rainy day an excuse to skip practice. The shot putter or discus thrower who has not had the experience of throwing from a rather wet, slippery circle, is often a very unhappy young man when he finds that he must do so in a state meet or some other important competition which must be run, rain or shine. Even the athlete who has practiced in the rain and knows what it is like to throw a slippery discus is not likely to enjoy the competition under such conditions, but he is not likely to be nearly as upset as the one who has avoided such experience (Figure 45).

Figure 45

DOUGHERTY OF CONCORD H.S. MEETING ADVERSE CONDITIONS.

But it is not only in field events that preparation for adverse conditions can pay off. Though most coaches are likely to warn their middle distance and distance runners to avoid leading for long stretches on days that are very windy, few actually make plans for such eventualities. Still fewer seem to have these runners practice running using the shelter of their own team mates under such conditions. It seems to me that there is something to be gained by deliberately planning to have one of your weaker runners take over the lead early in the race, especially along the stretches that must be run against a strong wind. The runner whom you count on to score should move into position just behind and off the shoulder of his team mate. He will thus avoid the extra burden of shielding his opponents from the wind.

Of all the running events in track, perhaps none is more affected by adverse wind conditions than the hurdle races, yet seldom is there any attention given to preparing for such conditions. Often I have stood quietly by and heard coaches and athletes moaning about their troubles when they find that a following wind has them too close to the hurdle at take-off or that a strong wind against the hurdler has him straining to cover the distance between hurdles in the required number of strides. I wonder sometimes whether the coach has even bothered to suggest to his hurdler that his trouble really stems from the wind conditions. I am convinced that the coach should not only remind the hurdler of the effects of such wind conditions but also arrange practices in which the athlete is working under both types of difficulty.

HURDLING AGAINST A STRONG WIND

Only when the coach has studied the technique of high hurdling carefully is he likely to realize just how troublesome a strong wind in the hurdler's face can be. Let me add one more warning: the shorter the hurdler, the more certain he is to have troubles when running against a strong wind. Unfortunately, some coaches think that once they have their hurdlers taking the necessary three steps between the highs they need only concentrate upon form over the hurdle to bring the boy to success. The truth is that many a hurdler who starts hitting hurdles or bounding between them in an effort to keep his three-stride spacing is meeting a problem for which he is unprepared.

Consider carefully what happens when an athlete is slowed up even slightly by a strong wind against him. Even his strides to the first hurdle are cut slightly. Although the difference may be only a few inches, these inches become mighty important to him as the race progresses. When he loses some of the momentum that his 15-yard sprint to the first hurdle has built up for him, he finds that this is only the forerunner of the effects between hurdles. He takes off for the first hurdle a few inches back of where he normally leaves the ground. Usually this will not bother the good hurdler too much. He will clear the barrier without too much trouble. But remember that when he lands after clearing he will be that same few inches behind his usual landing spot or he will be sailing farther through the air to reach it. Either way, he is in some trouble. As the race proceeds, the hurdler finds that he loses more ground to the wind. It is important to realize that between hurdles he has only three strides in which to build up the speed to carry him over each barrier. With a strong wind bucking him, he will find that he loses more and more ground until his hurdling rhythm is seriously affected.

The coach who is really on the job will not wait for the day of the big race to prepare his hurdler for his problem. He will make that hurdler do plenty of practicing against a strong wind. He will point out to him that under such conditions he must make an extra effort to keep his normal sprint strides to the first hurdle and even more to work up top speed between hurdles.

Even an extra strong following wind can be a real problem. Under such conditions, the hurdler finds that he is a little closer to the first hurdle than he normally is and therefore he must drive upward a little more than usual to clear the hurdle. Furthermore, since he is moving faster than usual to the first hurdle, he runs into trouble getting his lead leg up fast enough to clear. Some coaches fail to realize that a strong following wind can be very troublesome to a good hurdler. The solution to the problem is not in having the boy chop his strides to allow him clearance room. The emphasis should be upon having him concentrate upon getting his lead foot up *very* fast. Remember that he has less time than he expects to get that foot up and over the hurdle because he is moving faster than usual. If this were not true do you think that records set with the help of a following wind in any sprint or hurdle race would not be allowed? Adverse wind conditions will bother your hurdler far less if you have him practicing frequently both with and against a strong wind.

PLANNING RELAY PASSES FOR PROBLEM AREAS

Sometimes conditions at the site of a big meet, if you have failed to make necessary preparations for them, can have serious effects upon the success of your relay teams. You may be a coach who is anxious to give your relay team every legal advantage, and therefore you may have worked hard with them perfecting baton exchanges using the so-called inside pass. But if the track on which your team will compete is bordered by a fence or wall close to the inside of the track, you may be in for trouble if you draw the usually desirable inside lane. Your incoming runner will find that if he uses the right- to left-hand or "inside" pass, he will find little or no running room to the inside of the track after he has completed the pass. He may even be in danger of crashing into the fence or wall and injuring himself. With this in mind you may be wise to have your team work out ahead of time using the traditional left to right exchange of the baton. It is such advance planning and preparation that can save you not just a race but even the services of a runner.

PLANNING FOR INDOOR RACING CONDITIONS

Although in past years unusual conditions affecting indoor meets run on armory floors were problems only for coaches of indoor teams in the East, many areas have recently gone in more for indoor track using such surfaces. If you are a coach who must prepare your team for such indoor areas, you will be smart to study adverse conditions in such races as the dash, the 300 yard run, the sprint relays, and the hurdles. In most armories the runners will not be able to use starting blocks because authorities will not allow spikes to be driven into the floors. All sprint starts and all hurdle starts are definitely affected by such restrictions. You will have to prepare your sprinters and hurdlers by having them practice starts from flat surfaces. The placement of the feet in the bunch start with the feet well under the body is almost mandatory. The sprinter or hurdler must get all of his drive from the flat surface. He cannot push against starting blocks, so that if he tries to place his feet in an elongated starting position he will find that they slip from under him. For a sprinter, this is bad enough, but for a hurdler it is disastrous. The sprinter will get a poor start and still, if he is good enough, be able to make it up before the finish line, but the hurdler will find his steps to the first hurdle badly off. He is bound to be in trouble between hurdles as a result of his slip at the start. The coach should therefore give his sprinters and hurdlers plenty of starts from the bunch or semi-bunch position to help them learn how to start from flat surfaces.

Runners in the sprint relay starting leg must also be prepared to start from the flat surface, and if the 300-yard run is contested in your meets, you have the starting problem and another serious one also. There is the battle for the first turn or the first bank depending upon the conditions under which your boys race. You must therefore coach your boys to make an all-out effort to reach the first turn in the lead. In most cases the boy winning the race to the first turn is in command of the whole race. The others must drop behind him or risk running high on the bank or wide on the turn. Either means lost ground. You must also make clear to your boys that the nature of the indoor track restricts the possibilities for passing. There are usually no long straightaways like those on outdoor tracks so that passing must be accomplished in stretches of about 50 or 60 yards between banks or turns. These are specialized racing conditions for which you must prepare your runners if they are to be successful.

SOME SEEMING TRIVIA

If you happen to be a high school or college coach who has a runner good enough to compete in the national meets in various parts of the country or in other countries, you are going to have to consider another sort of problem which might be listed under adverse conditions. Many coaches and athletes are discovering that rapid flights from one section of the country to another are having unexpected effects upon competition. The eating and sleeping habits are being affected most. Athletes are finding that their bodies do not accustom themselves to the disrupted day and night sequences rapidly enough to permit top performances after such rapid changes. They are finding that flying ahead of the sun may be one of the modern miracles of travel by plane, but that the body cycle of hours for meals and rest is not adjusted so rapidly.

A little thought about this problem may make it more understandable. Any man who has ever taken on a job working nights after having worked days most of his life is likely to remember how long it took him to adjust to his new schedule. If he did not find sleeping in the daytime too difficult to adjust to, he undoubtedly found his eating habits seriously disturbed. In a lesser way, the athlete who flies across the country or from one country to another is meeting the same problem. As jet planes bring all sections of the country and even of the world closer together, the athlete making these hops from one area to another is going to have to consider the effects upon his body. It is not only climatic conditions that must be considered; it is also the need of giving the body time to prepare for its new environment.

Some coaches have already been farsighted enough to prepare their athletes for unusual conditions. Coach Thompson of England, considering the extraordinary humidity and heat under which the Rome Olympics might be competed, actually had members of the walking team spend long periods in steam baths to prepare them for conditions to be met in the Olympics. Some American coaches of swimmers had their charges working out under similar conditions. I believe that as records get better and better, coaches are going to recognize the value of preparing their track athletes for such adverse conditions. Just as coaches are realizing the need of special preparations for distance runners who are facing the demands of such altitudes as those of Mexico City, I predict that they will become more and more aware of the importance of preparing for climatic differences.

Many of the coaches of runners who were likely to compete in distance races in the 1968 Olympics were putting pressure upon the authorities to schedule such events as the marathon, the 10,000-meter run and others for late in the day so that the expected heat of Mexico City might not prove so troublesome to the runners. It is my belief that in the future we shall see much greater concern about such matters.

Already, some coaches have learned that distance runners who have been training at high altitudes are likely to run faster times than ever when brought to competition in areas close to sea level. The time may not be too far away when many more coaches are going to plan such training for their stars as they attempt to set new world's records.

I will go a step further and suggest that some field event coaches will be forced to consider such slight advantages for their throwers and jumpers as may be gained by competing in areas close to the equator. Unless the rules governing the long jump are liberalized in future years, coaches are going to think in terms of the inches gained by jumping in a country like Ecuador as opposed to one like New Zealand or countries far from the equator. When one recalls how relatively small the change in the world's record in the long jump had been in the past 30 years, until Beamon's jump in Mexico City, he is bound to recognize how important extra inches are in that event. Between 29 and 30 feet, the inches will come hard. Though there seems to be far more room for improvement in the triple jump, the effects of the pull of gravity close to and away from the equator are some day going to become an important consideration for the jumper with a world's record in mind. Again, note the amazing triple jumping in Mexico City. The little differences may well become the big differences in the future.

| Chapter 10 | MEETING THE OPPONENT'S PSYCHOLOGY |

Even when an athlete supposedly far superior to the field takes his marks or steps up to meet opponents in his event, there is always a bit of drama and uncertainty in the air. I can recall talking with Gil Dodds some years ago when he was America's top miler about his feelings as he stepped to the starting line. I was surprised then, though I am not now, to hear him say that he never stepped to the line without a little twinge of apprehension, no matter how mediocre the field. I remember quite well the attitude of respect that Gil accorded any opponent who entered a race against him. He seemed to know the times that many had run in previous races, and even though they might be several seconds slower than his usual winning times, he never took such men lightly as threats. Gil carried his laurels as one of the world's greatest milers of his day as gallantly as any champion I have ever met, and I have met many of them. I never once heard him belittle an opponent, even a scared college freshman running with the big boys for the first time. He was courteous, respectful, and never condescending.

One special incident stands out in my mind. I happened to have running for me at the time an outstanding boy, one who later became a national champion and record holder. Having no indoor track to work on, I frequently took the boy and several others not so great over to the Boston

College board track where Gil frequently worked out under the late Jack Ryder. Gil at the time was working on quarter miles to prepare for one of his big mile races. Always friendly, Gil watched my star work through some fast quarters and shook his head, remarking seriously, "Too fast for me!" Then he turned to me as I was about to put some of my lesser runners through some quarters and asked, "Skip, do you have a couple of boys who will be trying to hit 64 or 65 seconds? If so do you think they would mind if I ran with them?" I'm sure that you can imagine the look on the faces of my two 1:25-second 600 yarders, both of whom had seen Gil race to wins in 4:06 or thereabouts in the Boston Garden only a few nights before. But that was not all. When the two boys stepped to the starting line with him, he asked me which of the two was the faster and then turned to that boy and said, "Son, if I'm moving out too slowly for you, don't hesitate to take over and I'll let you set the pace." The boy looked at me, wide-eyed as you can imagine, and gasped, "Is he kidding?" But, knowing Gil, I could answer honestly and did, "No, he isn't." To me, it was tremendously significant that he was *not* kidding.

I recall that after the workout, Gil made a special point of coming over to the boys who had run with him and thanking them for their help as well as complimenting them on their good pace judgment. I wish that I could finish this little story by telling you that the two boys went on to become champions. They didn't, but they did improve and managed to score points for us in championship meets later. I can assure you that those boys and the others watching learned two important lessons that day. First they learned the value of pace judgment from a man who was a master of it. But they learned from him what seems to me an even more valuable lesson, *to respect others*.

RESPECT YOUR OPPONENT'S ABILITY

My purpose in relating this incident is not merely to pay tribute to a great runner whose records have long ago fallen to other great champions, but to emphasize the point that I consider most important in meeting your opponent's psychology. *Have a wholesome respect for any opponent*. Don't make the mistake of underestimating or belittling any man in your race. Especially in a championship race, every man entered has probably earned his way there by at least one good performance during the season. Echoing the thoughts of Gil Dodds again, let me remind you that you can never be sure that he may not be determined to make *this* race an even better one.

If you happen to be the defending champion, you have an added reason to respect your opponents. You can be sure that for some of them you are the target for the day. The emotions of competitors contribute greatly to the drama of any sport, but to none more than track. I am sure that any coach can recall instance after instance of champions so absorbed in their expected battle with top opponents that they awoke too late to the more serious threat of the unpublicized runner who had made up his mind that this was *his* day. As long as men continue to rise to challenge, there will always be a Billy Mills, a Mike Larrabee, or a Bob Schul. To make the mistake of underrating any opponent in the seeded heat of any race can be fatal. There is nothing wrong with a little wholesome fear of all who face you, *especially* in a championship race.

SOME FEAR IS NOT FOLLY

Obviously, I am not trying to tell you that you should go into every important race scared to death of your opponents. But on the other hand the man who has never known fear is a fool. Fear in some form is always with us. It is, in fact, a protective feeling. How the athlete reacts to it is what is important.

RACING STRATEGY AS MOTIVATION

Quite often a distance runner will go into a race fearing that he will be unable to finish if he sets a fast early pace, one that may be necessary in order to defeat a strong opponent. The coach can do such an athlete a great deal of good psychologically if he can persuade him that all athletes feel tired and spent long before they really are. I have always felt that giving such a runner a somewhat carefully planned race pattern to follow will help him by focusing his attention upon other things at critical stages of the race. If he can be led to concentrate upon racing strategy, he will have less time to worry about his feeling of fatigue. If he can be prepared for making scheduled moves at given stages of the race, he will be thinking positively rather than negatively at such points.

In high school meets, and in many college meets as well, athletes are often upset by opponents who tell them of times they have recently run or distances or heights they have achieved. Quite often such opponents are trying to do the very thing that they accomplish. They want to instill a little fear in those who must compete against them. Their air is usually one of confidence; yet often their boast is itself a sign of fear. You should make your boys realize that the pretended confidence is just that, *pretended confidence.* Your athlete should not let himself be disturbed by such a trick. Instead he should be encouraged to come right back at his opponents with a recital of some of his own recent times or distances. This particular trick works both ways.

It will be even more helpful to your boy if you can have him react with controlled anger to the threat offered by such an opponent. The reaction to anger can and often does delay fatigue because the athlete is filled with determination to prove himself against an opponent who has aroused that anger. That killer instinct so often talked about in great athletes, from boxers and football players to tennis players and track men, is no myth. It can and often does lead to exceptional performances by the athletes aroused. Coaches use all sorts of tricks to bring athletes to a fighting pitch, some of them very corny and some very subtle. The coach who doesn't go in for weekly heroics in the locker room may find that taking a boy aside and needling him into anger against a strong opponent who has belittled him will often send the boy out to the track ready for head-to-head confrontation with that opponent. I have found that having a boy's teammates go to him, one or two at a time, to work on him before such a race can be very effective in getting him up for the race. The coach can use this approach to avoid making his own personal approach to the athletes too frequent. The coach who seldom gives pep talks to groups or individuals can create quite a stir among them when he does. The ineffectiveness of the coach who rants and raves at his team every meet is quite obvious. The choice of time and place is important.

Except in preparation for unusual situations, the coach should realize that the type of anger needed for exceptional performance cannot be sustained for long periods. To start working on a squad or an individual early in the week and continue this day after day is a difficult thing to do effectively. There is a great deal of truth in the claim that the fight can be left on the practice field. You may be the type of coach who can begin early in the week of the big test to start that little flare of anger in the boy on Monday and fan it to a flame gradually by Saturday, but this is no mean trick. It takes care and knowledge of the boy as well as some understanding of pure mob psychology. Whether you build up the boy's anger against his chief opponents through a gradual process over several days or wait until the hour of the big race to work on him, you must remember that your one purpose is to send him to the line fired up with the thought, "I *won't* be beaten."

It has always seemed to me that one of a track coach's greatest assets must be the ability to arouse or inspire his athletes to unusual performance. Hundreds of coaches in all corners of the world know the techniques of events thoroughly. But after teaching the basics of an event, the coach must still get his athlete to perform better than the athlete believes that he can. Bringing an athlete or a team "up" for a critical test can be the coach's final contribution to the making of a champion.

FAITH IN ONE'S OWN ABILITY

The coach should realize that the athlete who starts thinking long and seriously about the good points of his opponent and comparing them with his own may end by fearing him more. I feel that it is better for the coach to focus the athlete's attention on the phases of his event in which he seems superior to his opponent. If he has the ability to get out in front in the race while his opponent likes to lie back and strike in the late stages, I try to get him thinking positively about his own strengths. I try to direct his anger and determination toward killing off his opponent's threat by using his fine opening speed to get out of the pack quickly and, if it is a middle distance or distance run, to control the early pace so that his opponent will be worried about lying back too far or too long. If the race is of shorter distance and several heats must be run, I like to have my sprinter or hurdler shake up his opponent by turning in a very good time in *one* of the heats, especially one that he is seeded in and is confident of winning easily. If the athlete is a jumper or pole vaulter, I will often have him concentrate upon deliberately clearing the cross bar by wide margins once or twice in the early competition. If he can do this and make it look easy, he will often affect the performance of good but jittery opponents. Whether the number of misses will be considered in determining a winner or not, I constantly urge my jumpers and vaulters to make every effort to clear on first try. I have no patience with athletes who waste trials through careless performances.

Some athletes who are disturbed about their own tenseness before a meet and during early competition need most to realize that by worrying about their opponents too much they are actually contributing toward their own defeat. No matter how he feels, the athlete should appear self confident to his opponents. If he can act self confidently, he will tend to build up his own confidence.

TACTICS IN EARLY STAGES OF THE EVENTS

If the athlete has prepared well and has worked on form improvement in his event, he will find that he is able to sustain good form even when he is having a bad day. If he maintains an air of confidence and exhibits good form, some of his opponents who are looking for signs of worry and weakness in him will begin to lose confidence in themselves. On the other hand, your athlete should be reminded that his opponents who look so composed and sure of themselves are not necessarily so. By close observation, your own athlete should be quick to spot over-confidence and take full advantage of it. There is nobody so ripe for the taking as a cocky, over-confident athlete. Surprise tactics that upset his race plans can be quickly demoralizing to the overconfident athlete who underrates his opponents.

Chapter 11

PREPPING THE TEAM FOR A CHAMPIONSHIP

ALMOST EVERY TRACK COACH WHO HAS WORKED HARD putting a strong team together sees them first developing into a strong dual meet team and then begins to wonder about their chance of becoming state champions. If he sees the state title as a bit too much for them, he may start thinking about their possibilities as league champions. If he has yet to coach his first championship team, he is getting ready for his first big thrill or his first big disappointment. The first thing that he needs to realize is that his strong dual meet team is not necessarily a serious threat in any title meet involving a fairly large number of teams. But he should also know that the depth that brought him so many wins in dual meet competition *may* be the very factor that can bring him his championship, even though he may see only one or two possible gold medal winners on his whole squad. There is a great deal of truth in the comment that coaches can win championships on the entry blanks.

Of the many championships that my teams have won, I can say honestly that more than half of them were taken by teams that were just too strong for our opponents to handle. In the words of so many coaches today, we had the horses. When your team can pile up over 50 points in a multi-school meet, while the best your nearest rival can do is about 20 points, you don't have to worry very much about placing your men to get every possible point. The boys do the winning and you take the bows.

But I can be just as honest in saying that several others were won through a combination of good luck and careful planning. In the language of coaches, some others I "stole." I did nothing underhanded or illegal, but I did study the strengths and weaknesses of my opponents very carefully and I definitely took advantage of them. I feel that the boys will sometimes make a coach look good by coming through for him when he has pulled a boner, but I also believe that if the coach is worth his salt he will at other times juggle the members of his team so that they contribute more points to the team cause than they could normally score.

"WINNING ON PAPER"

If your team is a standout, and you simply outclass the field, enjoy yourself; the feeling is wonderful, but one that some coaches never enjoy in a coaching lifetime. If you see the championship fight looming up as a dog fight with one or two points likely to determine the champion, I urge you to give long and careful thought to that entry blank. You *can win on paper*. Make the right entries and you're in; make the wrong ones and you're out.

THE PSYCHOLOGY OF ANTICIPATION

If you have some idea that I have always made the right moves and won, let me hasten to correct you. I think that I won meets that I should not have won, but I want to tip my hat here and publicly to some coaches who made me eat crow. Many of my teams will recall that I talked quietly with them before championship meets, telling them of possible moves by opposing coaches. I summed up our weaknesses and told them that if I were coaching against them, I would immediately make certain moves. I stressed to them that if the opposing coach failed to make such moves, we were better off than we expected to be. I warned them that if the coach was smart, he would see our weakness and do his best to take advantage of it, but that other moves that I had made might offset the very moves that he wisely made. I always felt that being honest with my contending teams was wise because it took away the shock that might otherwise come from the shrewd move of a good coach. I recommend that you do the same with your possible champions. If the opposing coaches *do* make the moves that take advantage of your team's weakness, you lose nothing because you have already prepared your team for such a possibility. If the coaches do *not* make the moves to exploit your team's weakness, you will bolster the confidence of your team because they will be quick to realize that an opponent has overlooked a weakness that they recognize. If I may digress a bit here, I want to say that part of the fun I got out of a long coaching career came from seeing young coaches spot my teams' weaknesses and take advantage of them. In a way, they made me look good to my own teams because they spotted the weaknesses that I told my boys we had. I have never enjoyed defeat and I guess that I never will take it easily, but I will admit that I felt a grudging admiration for the young coach who proved that he was a real student of track and was smart enough to spot the weaknesses in my team. So I urge you again, if you have a championship possibility, study your opponents from sprint to shot put. Look for weak spots as carefully as any football coach would study a weakness in his opponent's defense, and consider every move that you can make to take advantage of that weakness.

Another thing that any coach of a championship contender should realize is that he has something strong going for him. Ordinarily, the morale of a winning team is high and the chances are that its members will rise to the occasion when the title is at stake. Though it would seem quite obvious that a coach should use this momentum to prepare his team for a top effort, I have seen coaches lose great opportunities because they did not do so.

THE VALUE OF EARLY PLANNING

Very often a coach can see his team's championship possibilities early in the season. When he can assess the strength of his team realistically early in the year, he should begin working for that championship at once. From a careful study of the scorers who will be back in contention for his rivals in the coming title battle, the coach should form some estimate of the events which will be most open for scoring. He should make a long-range plan which will include covering all events possible yet concentrating his strength in events where points seem most available. True, the coach, as the season rolls along, may have to review the field and possibly make some changes to meet unexpected strength found among the new athletes on rival teams. But if he has made an early appraisal of strength in the various events, he will have a better chance to prepare his own team for scoring in events in which points may be up for grabs. Certainly, his early study of returning scorers should usually show him what events will be hardest for his team to score in. If he can spot standout athletes in several events, he should know that he may be sacrificing his team's chances by entering good men against the stars. Yes, there is always the possibility that the "sure" winner will fold in the stretch, turn up ill on the day of the meet, or upon some whim of his own or his coach be entered in another event. But these are only slim chances over which the coach eyeing the title can have no control.

POSSIBILITIES OF IMPROVEMENT IN EVENTS

Once the coach has checked on the returning scorers in all events to see where the threats lie and has assessed his own team honestly, he should decide how much improvement he can realistically expect from the boys on his squad. It is on this point that I believe many coaches make mistakes. They do more dreaming than reasoning. The coach who knows that the returning scorers in an event such as the discus throw include five or six boys who have thrown around 150 feet while his best thrower is doing only about 125 feet, is quite a dreamer if he expects his boy to improve 30 feet in a season while the others just stand still. Yet if such a coach expects points in the discus throw, this is just what will have to happen. I know that dramatic improvement is possible, but if I were such a coach I would not be counting points for my team in the discus. Knowledge of the opposition and honest analysis of the talent he has available are two mighty important factors in striking for a team championship. Add to these two factors some recognition of the probable limits of improvement for athletes in given events and you have before you three things that will usually reveal your real chances for a championship. The coach must ask himself, "How good are the athletes my boys must beat to score and on whose teams are they?" He must follow this with the question, "How much talent do I have available on my own team and in what events do I have it?" Then he has to ask himself, "How much improvement is *probable* in given events?" He knows that he cannot avoid the opposition, that he cannot make talent where there is none, and that only reasonable improvement can be anticipated in any event during a single season.

POSSIBLE IMPROVEMENT IN HURDLES

Some events are of such a nature that an athlete's possible improvement in them can be predicted quite accurately. The high hurdle race is such an event. If you as a coach are considering the chances of your good hurdlers developing into the best, you had better take a good close check on two things. First give him a sprint timing over the full distance of his race. Then time him over the hurdles for the same distance. If you find that your hurdler can sprint the 120 yards in about 13 seconds and complete the flight of hurdles in 16 seconds, you have some cold facts to face. If you do a great job of teaching him to hurdle, you can cut his total time over the hurdles from the three seconds that it now takes him to about 2.5 seconds. It is even possible that you may have that rare individual who can so improve his hurdling that he may clear the ten obstacles in close to two seconds. But even assuming that he becomes a model hurdler, you have yourself a 15-second high hurdler. You might cut a tenth of a second or so from his sprint time, but you had better realize that his chances of hitting 14.5 are mighty slim indeed. If points in the championship meet can be won only by breaking 15 seconds in the hurdles, then don't count too heavily upon any points that your hurdler can get you. Yes, it is quite possible that troubles may befall some of his opponents. The hurdle race is one in which many competitors come to grief. Even Harrison Dillard, one of the greatest of all time, found that out in an Olympic trial race. But barring accidents, your hurdler must be recognized as only an outside scoring possibility. His basic speed for the distance sets his limits. You can't perform miracles. On the other hand, if you have a boy who can do about 12 seconds for his 120 yards, you have a boy who is a definite prospect for under 14.5 when his hurdle clearance is perfected.

SPRINTERS SHOW LIMITED IMPROVEMENT

Any coach who is counting upon his sprinters to score in a championship meet later in the season needs to consider the calibre of the sprinters that his athletes must defeat and the capabilities of his own sprinters as he checks them over the distance early in the season. If he finds that the field includes several 10-second sprinters, and he realizes that his best man runs about 10.5, he must be realistic enough to admit that dramatic improvement in sprinters is not a usual thing. During a single season, an improvement of three-tenths of a second is quite an achievement. More frequently the coach will find that his sprinter will be only one or two tenths of a second faster at the end of a season than he was at the beginning. Sometimes, even that slight improvement is not found. Nobody has yet proved that the long-held belief that sprinters are born, not made, is false. All that a coach can hope to do is to assist his sprinter to use the speed that God has given him. The coach can make his starting more efficient, correct any flaws in arm action, head position, or foot placement, and help the boy to build stamina to maintain his speed to its maximum limit. He cannot create speed where there is none nor add significantly to the speed that any sprinter has.

IMPROVEMENT OF DISTANCE RUNNERS

I confess that I have never been swayed from my belief that distance running talent is just as positive a natural thing as sprint talent is. I have never been convinced that just any runner can become a great miler or two miler or cross country star. I firmly believe that distance running promise is detectable among high school runners. I have seen too many boys who have never run track turn in surprising times in intramural mile races. or novice cross country runs to accept the idea that any person can make himself into a top flight distance runner. I can't accept that any more than I can the notion that any boy who wants to be a Bob Cousy in basketball can be one or that any boy who wants to be a Sandy Koufax in baseball can do so. Natural talent must be involved.

For the coach looking ahead toward a possible championship, there is something to be said in favor of the distance runs as scoring possibilities. The room for development in distance runners far exceeds that for sprinters. Yet that very possibility makes it more important that the coach begin work far ahead of the date of the championship meet. It is ridiculous to start a "crash" program for distance runners three or four weeks before the championship day. Unless your distance runner has been preparing for months, not weeks, he will show no great improvement on the day of the big race. It is definitely possible to chop many seconds off the runner's time in the mile or two-mile run, but not without a carefully planned background which includes a long period of running for months getting both the body and the mind ready for all-out effort by subjecting it to constant stress. Many high school and college distance runners short-change themselves during this stage of their training. If you as a coach have been foresighted enough to build up the strength and endurance of your distance men with a careful program of weight training and long distance running, you will find them ready for the speed work and hard interval training that should be a part of their sharpening for the all-important meet.

Perhaps the events in which most dramatic improvement can be seen are the high jump and the pole vault. It seems to me that coaches often overlook these events as promising point getters in championship meets. If I had to decide which events would pay off best for concentrated coaching effort, I would take a long look at the prospective competition in the high jump, the pole vault and the hurdles. In all my coaching career, I cannot recall one 11-second sprinter that I brought down to 10 seconds in the course of any season. In fact I cannot recall any coach that I know who can point to any such dramatic improvement. There may be some who can make that claim, but they must know some secret about sprint training that most of us don't know. I have, on the other hand, taken high jumpers from five feet to close to six feet in a season. I have had pole vaulters go from nine feet to eleven feet in just a few weeks. I have had high hurdlers cut a full second off their early season times by the time of the big meets. Any coach who is seriously after a championship should be aware of *where he can take points away from his chief rivals for the title.*

CONSIDER PACKING A WEAK EVENT

One of the mistakes some coaches make in planning a drive for a championship is to spread their talent too thinly. Whenever the meet rules allow it, I am strong for packing weak events with good scoring possibilities. You can give your rivals quite a shock early in the meet if you can hit them with two or three scorers in a single event. This is possible far more often than many coaches realize. It might be interesting for you as a coach to check up on the entry lists in past years in such events as the high hurdles in your championship meets. My guess is that you will find the actual entry list far shorter than that in either the 100-yard run or the 220. If you do your home work well and check out the hurdlers who actually stepped to the starting line, you may get quite a surprise. Often the hurdle field checked in is so small that only heats and finals are necessary. Semifinals often do not have to be run. The coach who overlooks such scoring possibilities is not really preparing his team for its best effort.

LET SOME EVENTS ALONE

I am convinced that a coach's astuteness sometimes shows just as clearly in the events that he lets alone as in those in which he enters his boys. Oh, I believe that every coach should cover every event when that is possible, but when qualifying times and distances must be submitted to entitle the boys to compete in the championship events, I think that coaches often overlook an obvious possibility. The coach who has a fairly good miler should consider having that boy run the 880 or two mile in some meets so that he will have qualifying times in two or three events. You make life much easier for your rival coaches when they know that your boy has qualified in only one event. You can shake them up a bit by having him as a possible entry in one or two others. You give yourself the opportunity to shift. They then must make the right guess about where you will run him in the big meet.

CONSIDER THE IMPORTANCE OF SEEDING

One of the most enlightening experiences that a coach can have is that of shouldering the responsibility of directing a big invitational or championship meet. I have directed many of them and it has always amazed me to see how the laxness of a coach can cost him a meet even before it starts. Even when coaches are warned to star outstanding entries for seeding purposes, they do not do so. Though you may find it difficult to believe, some actually do leave out the names of their best athletes and fail to realize it. Some will deliberately turn in qualifying times worse than their boys have achieved without giving a thought to what this will mean during the seeding of heats. The coach who knows that his star will run a better race if he can get clear of the field quickly may be entirely justified in keeping that boy out of the seeded heat. If he is a real "front runner," it is often a smart move to have him in an event against unseeded runners whom he can outdistance early. The coach must realize, however, that his runner will have to make the racing pace, and unless he does so effectively, he may find that his time is not good enough to put him among the scorers.

THE SIGNIFICANCE OF SEEDINGS

If the seeding committee will be placing boys according to their best qualifying times, the coach must see to it that his boy some time during the season turns in a top effort regardless of the ease with which he may be winning his dual meets. If the coach fails to do this or fails to submit the boy's best qualifying time, he has only himself to blame if the boy is not placed in a seeded heat.

Seeding in championship meets is extremely important in events such as the hurdles or dashes and equally so in the sprint relays. Whether your good hurdler or sprinter finds himself racing several others just as good or is in a seeded heat that protects him is often up to his coach. The coach who fails to star his good hurdler or sprinter when asked to do so is not doing his part in getting his team ready for a championship effort.

Though there is nothing very new or startling about such a move, the coach searching frantically for the extra two or three points that may mean the championship may be making a smart decision if he holds one or two good boys out of the sprint events to have them fresh for the relay. I have been surprised at times to see coaches running sprinters in heats and quarter finals of a 220 when it was obvious that they had very little hope of getting into the finals, yet throwing those same boys back into an 880-yard relay a little later. It seems to me that in such instances the coach could be wasting boys in an event in which they had little hope of scoring and overlooking the advantage that he might have in the relay by having those boys fresh and strong.

MAKING USE OF MEET RULES

Still another factor in championship meets that coaches are likely to overlook is the variance in rules under which different meets are conducted. As director of a meet, I have often had a coach come up to me after an event and comment about a meet rule which he claimed to be unaware of. He would be saying this in spite of the fact that the rule was clearly stated on the entry blank and even mentioned specifically in a letter accompanying the entry blank. Coaches fighting for a team championship have little excuse for such oversights. What is more important is that they are sometimes hurting their team's chances of winning.

One example of the sort of rule that many meets have and one which offers definite advantages to the alert coach is that which allows a boy to enter another event if eliminated in the trial heats of the dash or hurdles. Since many meets are run on the basis of one running event, one field event, and one relay, a boy normally will be in three events. Some of the larger meets permit him to compete in only two events, one running and one field. The coach who does not take advantage of the rule which allows his boy to compete in another running event if he is eliminated in earlier sprint or hurdle trials is overlooking scoring possibilities.

No matter how often directors of meets repeat their request to coaches to enter boys in order of ability in various running events, many fail to do so. Then on the day of the meet they are moaning all over the stadium because they find their top boys in slow heats and their inferior boys seeded. From my work with scores of seeding committees, I can assure coaches that the committees do an honest and often thankless job of setting up the heats in accordance with the information supplied on the entry blanks. Indeed, they will often protect an outstanding competitor whose coach has left him unprotected. This may seem hard to believe, but I have sat in a seeding meeting while the director of the meet phoned a coach who had failed to enter a boy who was rated a sure thing in his event. I have sat in other meetings where the director refused to call the coach in somewhat similar situations and left him in a mighty embarrassing spot. Unfortunately the boys and their teams were the ones really hurt by the coaches' failure.

As championship meets grow larger and larger, the directors are becoming more and more strict about the matter of late entries and late switches in events. Despite warnings in heavy type, coaches continue to enter boys in several running events and become upset when the director of the meet scratches their boys from all events except the first one listed on the entry blank. Not too long ago a rival of mine lost a championship to my team because he entered a boy in two events against the rules and found his boy ineligible to compete in the second event. He had stood watching while the first event, in which he was legally entered, went off. When I say that some coaches lose meets on the entry blanks, I *mean* just that.

PREPARING THE ATHLETE FOR THE EXTENDED MEET

In a final note of caution for coaches who are readying teams for real shots at championships, let me urge that the coach study thoroughly the conditions under which the meet is to be run. The coach who knows long in advance that his high hurdler must face a series of trials, quarter finals, semi-finals and finals to get into the scoring must realize that the boy faces a long day's work. He will be helping that boy immeasurably if several weeks before the championship meet, he has the boy doing plenty of over-distance hurdling, setting up flights of hurdles facing both ways on the track or better yet on the football field and having him run the hurdles up and back. It may be necessary to start the boy on a flight of 11 or 12 hurdles. Then as he grows stronger, he should be taking ten one way and five the other. It is difficult but possible for a strong hurdler to run the full flight down the field and then with a two-and-one-half minute rest run a full flight back up the field. Certainly the sprinting of 150's and 220's is a very important part of the build-up of the high hurdler who must face a long series of trials in the title meet.

What has been said about preparing for several trials in the hurdles applies just as much to the dashes and low hurdles. The coach who sees his boys cracking under the strain of repeated trials in the dashes and hurdles should realize that he does not have those boys ready to meet the conditions under which the championship is contested.

Perhaps most coaches do recognize and prepare for the conditions under which the meet will be run, insofar as preparing boys for the strain of repeated running events is concerned. It is not so evident that they give the same serious consideration to conditions to be met in the field events.

Outdoor meets certainly must be contested without any assurance that good weather will prevail. In the East, rain, wind, and cold weather greet many a meet. Rain-slicked discus and shot put circles, slippery grass approaches in the javelin throw along with wet implements themselves bother competitors. In my book a coach is very smart when he prepares his team for a championship by insisting that they practice under all sorts of weather conditions. The boy who has worked out on a wet, slippery discus circle or shot put circle is not likely to be upset so much as one who has avoided practice under such conditions. The javelin thrower who has experimented with various types of shoes to find out which will serve him best in rain or sunshine is ready for either when the big day comes. He is going to know the importance of keeping that discus as dry as possible and wiping it clean of bits of mud before he enters the circle to take his trials.

Many times I have heard hurdlers complain about having to run against the wind, especially if it is strong and cold. It seems to me that any coach who is counting upon his hurdlers to get him points in a championship meet is missing a bet if he does not insist upon his hurdlers' practicing hard on windy days with the wind against them. Any hurdler who has difficulty maintaining the speedy rhythm of his three strides between hurdles on calm days will find it difficult to adjust to a strong opposing wind. If he has not worked seriously at bucking the wind in a hurdle race, he is almost certain to be disturbed when he must meet such a condition in the championship meet.

Long jumpers and pole vaulters also find wind conditions very important in setting up their approach runs. Long jumpers seem more aware of this than pole vaulters do. The coach who is seeking to give all possible psychological assistance to his long jumpers should look upon the windy day as a factor in his favor. He should never miss the opportunity to have his jumpers work hard on such days to make any necessary adjustments in the approach run. A long jumper who has established his marks on a calm day and has real confidence in his ability to hit the take-off board exactly should be urged to take actual measurements of his approach run. He should realize, however, that even on calm days he must expect to make slight adjustments from runway to runway. He needs only a few practices to learn how much to move his marks in to compensate for a strong wind in his face. It is usually the boy with only a vague idea of his approach run who finds himself fouling repeatedly when conditions are bad. Nor should the coach or jumpers overlook the effects of a strong following wind upon the approach run. Many of the problems arising from wind conditions on the day of the meet can be handled by the coach's insistence that the jumpers think of those unpleasant days as real opportunities to gain advantage over their opponents.

Only recently I noticed a young pole vaulter with whom I have been working get himself into a real bind trying to straighten out his approach run while moving against a strong wind. He is a rather tense, explosive type of athlete anyway and he was giving himself quite a time because his steps were all fouled up. Until I walked over to him and spent a few minutes calming him and pointing out to him that he now had an opportunity to make approach run adjustments against the wind, he had been getting very little good out of the day's practice.

Because pole vaulters, unlike long jumpers, do not have a take-off board to hit, we are inclined to forget that their point of take-off is just as important as that of the long jumper. The pole vaulter who overstretches to hit his take-off mark is just as badly off as the long jumper who over-stretches to reach a take-off board. Frequently an opposing wind will cause a vaulter to shorten his stride slightly. Even though this may make only a couple of inches' difference in a stride, the total effect can be interesting by the time the boy attempts to plant the pole. Either he will find himself suddenly forced to add a choppy step or two to get into good take-off position, or he will be over-reaching and in very poor balance. The result will probably be a bad miss. The boy whose coach makes him aware of this difficulty and makes him recognize the usually undesirable windy day as a blessing in disguise is making his attempt at scoring in the title meet that much easier. Any coach and any team can use the weather as either an aid or a handicap.

Chapter 12	BREAKING THE LOSING STREAK

For EVERY COACH WHO HAS KNOWN THE EXCITEMENT OF trying to get a team keyed up for a drive to a championship, there is one who has had to face the discouraging task of trying to lift the morale of a team mired in a long losing streak. Motivation is important in both instances, but the need is different in each. Many times in my own coaching career I have felt the thrill of stimulating the good team as it made its bid for a championship. I hope that I contributed something toward the successes of more than 50 championship drives that my teams have made. I can assure you that I enjoyed to the utmost the thrill of winning, but I would be telling less than the truth if I gave you the impression that I have not felt the frustrations of the losing coach. I know the feeling of facing a season's schedule with a squad that I knew in my heart had very little hope of winning a single meet. One of the tributes that I treasure most in my coaching career is a remark from a rival coach after my team had beaten his and a couple more in a season that started out as a complete washout. He shook his head in disbelief and asked, "What in blazes did you feed those kids to get them *up* this high?" What I "fed" them is exactly what this chapter discloses.

THE PROBLEM OF NEW MORALE

If you are a coach caught in the throes of a long losing streak, you must realize first that the motivation that worked in your drive toward a championship will not be very effective now. Most teams battling for titles are "trembling for the trumpets." They are keyed up, flushed with success during their regular season, sometimes even undefeated. They are "up" already. Their morale is high; their confidence is strong. Your job may be one of preventing over-confidence. You may even have to work on calming them down, lest their over-eagerness and tenseness lead to trouble. The team caught in the midst of a losing streak is a much different problem. They have become somewhat accustomed to losing. They have often lost confidence in themselves, if they ever had any to lose. They need a real injection of *morale*. It is my contention that in this situation you face a tougher coaching job than any coach who tries to point his team for a championship.

Let's assume that you face a league schedule with a squad that you know in your heart hasn't a prayer against any of your opponents during the first three-fourths of the schedule. Your only hope is to edge out one of your later opponents, and even that may seem like an outside hope. What do you do about it?

ASSESSING YOUR TEAM'S CHANCES

You must begin by taking a good, honest look at your opponents and at your own squad. When you realize that what you have as talent is hopelessly outclassed by most of your rivals, you will gain nothing by Knute Rockne type pep talks and foolish insistence that your team can win in a walk. You will gain nothing by ranting and raving at your team when it goes down to an overwhelming defeat (as you knew it would). An old coaching friend of mine used to remark, "You can't expect a 55-second quarter miler to beat a 50-second quarter miler." Well, *usually* you can't. Certainly your ranting at him won't win for him after the race is over.

You look at your schedule and at your squad, and you *know* that you face a long, unhappy season. You can shrug your shoulders and wait for better days, or you can do something positive instead. *You can point for the logical win.* Let's assume that the fifth team you meet is one that just might be taken. Scout that team thoroughly and learn all that you can about it. Watch its members closely in their meets to determine their strengths and weaknesses. Remember that this meet may be the key to the end of your losing streak. Don't waste your time trying to fill your team with hokum about earlier meets that are completely out of their reach. Take the team members into your confidence and tell them the truth. The majority of the boys can see the handwriting on the wall. They know when they are outclassed. Have them think ahead to the meet that can be won. Stress the point that the meets that precede the critical one are merely testing grounds for the real battle. Oh, I know that there are some coaches who will argue that you should never admit defeat. My only answer to such coaches is, "Do you think that you can convince any five-foot high jumper that he is going to beat one who consistently jumps six feet?" Even your dreams must be based on reality.

I have had success in stimulating track athletes to outstanding performances on quite a few occasions. I am convinced that I had such success partially because these athletes knew that I was not selling them the impossible. To convince a team that it has a chance for victory and then have it swamped in the meet destroys the faith of boys in their coach. I have often gone over meets in advance with boys to show them point by point what their chances are. I indicate to them the places that really may be won without the aid of miracles. I prepare such a diagnosis very carefully and suggest that the probable score can be within a certain point range. I urge them to try to lower the strong team's margin of victory. If the team we are aiming to beat has already lost to the strong team by a big margin, I work on my team to strive for a less disastrous loss. In this way I try to make an actual defeat work toward the motivation of my team in its later effort to end the streak.

If my team succeeds in holding the strong team's margin of victory to less than that it ran up against our prospective victim, I caution my own team about bringing this up when talking to members of the team we are pointing to beat. When pointing for a certain meet to end a losing streak, have your boys avoid giving the team any advance warning. You'd be surprised how many coaches will see no particular significance in your team's loss to Team A by an 18-point margin when their loss was by a 20-point margin. But when you are alone with your team, dwell happily upon the two-point difference as one more sign that the long-awaited victory is in sight.

Don't stop the motivation with comments about team achievement. Whenever possible, single out performances by your own boys in various events that were better than those of their opponents against the same team. Praise every sign of improvement and stress the slight improvement still needed to bring victory in the events that show narrow advantages for boys on the team that you aim to defeat.

PLANNING THE WORKOUTS

Next, begin your plans for workouts that will assure the slight improvements needed. Have every practice session one that will bring encouragement to some members of your team. This is no time to assign hard, discouraging work schedules. You are trying to revive the morale of a team accustomed to defeat. If you can catch the boys in the spirit of the plan, you will find that their efforts *do* show improvement. Their renewed enthusiasm will lead to better performances. Don't miss the chance to praise every lowered time or added height or distance.

If your meets are run during the outdoor season, don't miss the opportunity to practice under unpleasant conditions. Make your squad see that practice in the rain, wind, or cold will prepare them for a meet under such conditions, should they occur on the day of your big bid for victory. Don't let your team have the weather as an excuse for poor performance. Remember, *this is your big chance.* You win this one or the season is a disaster. Point out to your squad that poor weather conditions may work in their favor if they face an opponent grumbling and discontented because the meet has to be run in unpleasant weather. Turn every possible handicap into a help.

If you are the type of coach who has that little knack of inspiring a squad, build up for the big day gradually. Don't fire them up for every meet and then find out that you must do the job over during the week of the big effort. Get the squad into the act too. Have your captain and your other veterans moving about, giving encouragement here and there, just as you do. Get the squad looking beyond the defeat which seems certain this week toward the meet that will end the famine, three weeks away. Tackle this assignment as determinedly as you would preparation for a championship.

During the weeks of preparation for the big try, work hard with the key individuals in your prospective victory. Give them more personal attention than usual. Make them feel that they are getting special help. I found that it was very important to work extra hard with those boys who performed *almost* on a par with their opponents, so that they might have that little bit extra when the chips were down. If the other jumper was doing 5'5" and mine was too, I would be making an extra effort to get him over 5'6" or 5'7" to give him that added bit of confidence that might bring those vital points. If my jumper already had a slight edge over his opponent, I would work with him to increase that edge, also with the hope of increasing his confidence and making his necessary points more certain.

HIDING YOUR STRENGTH

Under certain conditions you may find it wise to hide your real strength in early meets, even at the risk of taking worse beatings at the hands of the strong teams. Keeping your real miler hidden in the two-mile run or in the

880, you may gain a psychological advantage when you spot him where he belongs in the meet that you expect to win. Moves like this can cause real consternation among the boys on an opposing team. The coach who looks confidently toward a big edge in a particular event can get a rude jolt when you suddenly make the switch that spoils his plans. On the other hand, such strategy can raise the morale of your boy, who feels that his racing in the two mile is going to aid his endurance in the mile, or that working in the 880 will boost his speed for that big effort in the mile later. Naturally, such shifts should be planned only after careful analysis of your opponents' strengths and weaknesses and upon your conviction that the move will have a real chance of succeeding. This is the type of move that can backfire. If it does, be man enough to shoulder the blame yourself. If it works, you will deserve the credit; if it fails you deserve the blame. In any event, don't lose sight of the boost to morale which can result if the suggestion of the shift gets enthusiastic approval from the boy or boys involved.

As you study the possibilities in the big meet ahead, consider carefully the outstanding weaknesses in your rival team. There is more than a cliché involved in the advice, "Strike hard at weakness." Don't ever lose sight of the fact that in a dual meet the points you gain are points your opponent loses. If the rival coach is envisioning a 5-4 spread of points in the shot put and you turn up a boy who takes the third place that he expected, the spread then becomes 6-3. Unlike points in a major meet involving several schools, points in a dual meet must go to either your team or your rivals. This is a most obvious point, yet it is one that many coaches do not consider enough in planning a meet.

STIMULATING THE TEAM FOR THE BIG EFFORT

It would be most unwise to plot out your own moves for the meet without considering possible counter-moves by the opposing coach. Give him credit for some intelligence too. Try to figure out what moves you would make to strengthen your position if you were he. Sometimes in preparing for such a crucial meet, I have talked over with my own team certain moves that our opponents might make to strengthen themselves for our meet. I do this to give them an added lift on the day of the meet. If the coach does not make the moves that could hurt us, we see the failure as something working in our favor. If the coach proves his shrewdness by making the moves, we still gain because we rob him of the advantage of surprise. I have even gone a bit further at times. I have suggested that our opponents may know of some moves that may be advisable that we don't know. I remind my squad of some of our obvious weaknesses and the need for improvement, lest our opponent hit us hard where we are weakest. Sometimes there are no possible moves, so nothing can be done to employ this particular strategy.

Still another bit of strategy that can be prepared is a planned change in racing tactics. If you have a half miler who has been tabbed as one who likes to lie back and strike from behind in the last 220 of the race, consider the advisability of shaking up your opponents by spending the two or three weeks available to prepare the boy for a strong opening 660. High school boys who are not experienced runners can be badly shaken by an unexpected move of this sort. Planned moves like this one serve a double purpose. They sometimes disconcert opponents, and they quite often add to your boy's confidence because he is taking the offensive.

Perhaps one of the oldest tricks in the business is that of sending out a "rabbit" in a middle distance or distance race. The trick is so old, like the statue of liberty play in football, that sometimes it still works. Even when you use it without variations, it can trap a nervous opponent who is too jittery to keep his poise. Even in its outdated original form, it still can contribute to team morale. I mean by this that it makes the hopelessly outclassed runner on your team feel that he is contributing something toward the upset that you are planning. You may look upon this as individual motivation, but I think of it also as part of the team motivation. I like to get every boy on the team into the act. When I approach a boy with the suggestion that he sacrifice himself to help a teammate, I do so with some thought as to my selection and to how he can best contribute to the whole team effort. Take my advice and don't knock it until you try it. But *try* it with an *intelligent* boy who can follow directions, one who realizes that a poor act fools nobody.

Sometimes as you study the team you are aiming at, you discover that certain boys on the team show poor knowledge of pace. You notice that the team's best miler seems to fold in the late stages of a race if he tries to follow an early pace that is very fast. With this in mind, you can bait your trap. I suggest that you select one of your boys who can run a fair half mile, but who seems outclassed by those on the opposing team. He is a boy who is used to running a faster pace than the milers usually set so that his moving to the front at once and setting a slightly slower pace than he carries in the 880 will not arouse too much suspicion. This will be most effective if you have already pulled one upset by a switch that has paid off. Both the opposing coach and the other team's miler will be recalling the earlier upset and will therefore be uncertain of the wisdom of letting your runner get out there without a challenge. This is especially true if he can sustain his pace well into the third quarter of the race. Your good miler, aware of what is happening, should run under control and conserve his strength until late in the race when his chief rival has spent himself following the pace of your smart "rabbit."

You should make it clear to your "rabbit" that he is not to make one grand and glorious flourish that will take him out in front by 40 or 50 yards only to have him go wooden-legged halfway through the second quarter. Instead, have him try for a 20- or 25-yard lead that will be worrisome to the opponent and will still enable him to hold his pace at least halfway through the third quarter. Then if your opponent likes to ease up in *his* third quarter, he will be a little afraid to do so. Your own runner may well be aided by thinking of his racing plan rather than his aches and pains, and may be in better racing form than he expected to be at this point in the race. If the opposing miler picks up the pace much earlier than he normally would, you have accomplished all that you have a right to expect. Your own miler must lay off the pace until his opponent has spent some of his strength trying to cut down the lead of your "rabbit." Encourage that boy to hold off the opposing miler through the third quarter, if possible. If he finds the strength, he should fight off the opposing runner when he tries to pass. If your boy can fight him off even once, he will aid your own miler by taking that little extra out of the other team's top man. Then when your good miler makes his bid, perhaps in the final 220, he will be challenging a rival who has already had to fight off an earlier challenge or two. I have seen this make the all-important difference in a race.

There is one other gain possible. Sometimes your "rabbit," finding himself still in front with only a lap and a half to go, may prove to be fighter enough to hold on for a third place and an unexpected bonus point.

DISCUSSING THE MEET TACTICS

In getting your team up for the big try, don't neglect to warn them about possible reversals. Point out, when you can, the possible upsets that your opponents might score. Whenever I am handling this phase of the preparation, I try to present alternatives to offset the setbacks. I try my best to prevent a collapse merely because one or two things go wrong. I never deliberately overestimate our scoring possibilities. In fact, I am extremely conservative in my analysis of our scoring. I feel that it is wise to stress our *minimum* scoring possibilities whenever such scoring will emphasize the reasonableness of my expectations of the team. I try to point out that their scoring chances are greater than such a minimum so that their confidence will be boosted a bit.

As the day of the big test approaches, I work harder than ever to build up the morale of the team. I do this not only by personal encouragement but also by working on every member of the squad, urging each to yell encouragement to every performer during practice sessions. It is at this point that I start my final drive to get them "up" for the meet, but I do it by enlisting their assistance. I don't stop with encouraging only the key performers. I now do everything possible to make them think and act like a team. I stress the fact that everyone has something to contribute to this team effort. Nobody, and *I mean* NOBODY, is excluded. I start this drive during the final week of preparation, and I insist upon its being continued during the meet, once that gets under way.

I sometimes save something for that little extra motivation on the day of the meet. I have on occasions offered a school letter to every boy who scores in this one meet. I have found that the little extra incentive has a surprising influence upon boys who have little hope of scoring the points usually necessary for a school letter.

On the day of the meet, I have only a few basic comments to make to the team as a whole. I often make them on the bus as we go to the place of the meet or in the locker room before we take the field. Then I take the time to go over the critical points to be contested. Perhaps the 440 is one of the early events in which we must get a second and a third place to be on schedule. I call up beside me the two or three boys whom I have been grooming to help offset the loss of first place which seems inevitable. I stress calmly and confidently that these two or three boys are our first keys to the upset. I try my best to make them realize that their places are just as important to us as the first place we are counting on in another event. I make it a point to speak to the key boys in every event. I mention quietly their hard work during the practice, and stress such improvement as they may have shown. Oftentimes this means giving a personal talk to ten or twelve boys, many of whom will, at best contribute a single point toward our cause. I make it clear also that all of us are counting on a top performance from every single star. I remind them that we must expect a contest from our opponents and that their points are not certain until they win them.

I follow these individual "pep talks" with one more reminder which I consider extremely important, yet one overlooked by some coaches trying for an upset. I emphasize the importance of points picked up in the first two or three events. I remind my boys that such points are sometimes chalked up on our side of the board before the opposing team senses that it is in trouble. Quite often the opposing team will enter such a meet quite confident of a win and therefore will not be immediately aware of the importance of a point chipped away here and there early in the meet. Sometimes they will react too late and the meet is out of reach before they realize it.

I don't make this a longwinded speech but a crisp expression of confidence in every boy there.

I conclude the talk to the team by asking them to try for one quick upset to shake the morale of the opposing team. This may be in the mile if that event comes early in the meet. It may involve the special "rabbit" who has been prepared. We know that this is an event that our opponents count as in the bag, so if our attempt for the upset fails, we are no worse off than we might have been without trying it. If our "rabbit" holds on for a third place point, we have gained by the effort. We look upon this effort as possible insurance and do not count those points as essential in our pre-meet break down of critical points for our victory. If we get the points we are better off than we expected to be at the end of this event. If we lose them because our top miler proves unable to beat their top man, I am quick to point out that this was only a gamble that we took knowingly so we have not lost crucial points.

While the meet is in progress, I keep the team in touch with developments. They keep coming to me for word on how close to point expectations we are running. When we lose a point that we had counted on, I have seen boys hurry back to their teammates urging this one or that one to an extra effort to pick up the point that had been lost in an earlier event. If your job of motivation has been well done, you will find that you get much satisfaction from the atmosphere that surrounds your team on such an occasion. Even if things go wrong and you don't come up with a win, you will be a strange coach indeed if you don't realize that you have done a top-notch coaching job. You and your squad are winners even if you lose. And I'll bet my bottom dollar that you will often come out a winner in fact as well as in spirit.

Chapter 13	PREPARING FOR SPECIAL EVENTS

More and more often these days, even at the high school level, coaches are finding that events once seldom contested in high school or college are being introduced into their meets. The triple jump for years was seldom seen in meets in the United States, although it was frequently a part of meets in Canada. The steeple chase only a few years ago might be found in certain A.A.U. meets but almost never in college meets. The 440-yard hurdles hardly ever contested in college meets now is found in many of them, and is already being pushed to replace the low hurdles in high school meets. The hammer throw in high school meets could be found only in Rhode Island and still is found in few others. Only in Rhode Island on the East Coast and California on the West Coast do we find much hammer throwing at any level. But the pressure is being applied to have the 12-pound hammer throw introduced in several other states. Even the decathlon, an event that for years was heard of only at the time of the Olympic Games, is beginning to attract the interest of athletes on both the college and the high school levels. Ironically, I submit that you can still find many a coach who cannot tell you what events are included in a decathlon. But the ripples of interest are beginning to swell, and before long many more of us may find that we have to prepare athletes for competition in one or more of the events mentioned above.

In many states relay carnivals involving the use of *teams* of shot putters, *teams* of pole vaulters, *teams* of javelin throwers and of other field event men are beginning to be popular. As track and field squads grow larger and larger it is probable that such events will become more common than ever. The coach is going to have to develop teams of field event men to go along with his relay teams if he hopes to win one of these combined meets.

In one sense, such developments may prove a benefit to a coach, even though he may think of them as piling more of a burden upon him when he already considers himself over-loaded. The benefit I mean is that such meets may keep his weaker field event men interested because they will be able to score points as part of a team which includes the better athletes. I consider them very valuable psychologically because they lead to three or four field event men's thinking of themselves as a *team*. This sense of "belonging" is more of a spur to many young high school athletes than some coaches realize.

One of the benefits of such team events is their effect upon the good shot putters, or discus throwers, or high jumpers, who find that their own chances of winning medals demand more than their own effort. They find themselves assisting the lesser athletes and in effect becoming assistant coaches. In truth, the coach may find that he is accomplishing more with his team as a whole because the interest of field event groups within it has been heightened.

WORKING WITH BEGINNING TRIPLE JUMPERS

Perhaps the first event you may find added to your meet program will be the triple jump, if it is not already a recent addition. Many a high school coach will throw up his hands and kiss the points goodbye because he feels that he knows nothing about the event and is doubtful of his ability to coach boys in triple jumping. Most coaches immediately think of making one of their fairly good long jumpers into a triple jumper. There's really nothing wrong with such a decision, but there can be a great deal better chance of success if he chooses the right one. And the right one may not be your best long jumper. If you have ever noticed among your jumpers a boy who sometimes hits the take-off board with the wrong foot and still manages to get a creditable jump from it, you have a good clue to your best triple jump prospect. You should realize that while two of the phases of the triple jump involve take-offs from the strong foot, one phase demands a take-off from the so-called weak foot. Since you will eventually be trying to strengthen both legs of your triple jumper, you may save yourself time and frustration by starting with a boy who has already shown you that he can get a respectable jump from either foot.

When you start to work with such a candidate, you must realize that one of the things that you have been emphasizing to him in his long jumping must be changed. The long jumper is working in terms of a single landing. When his feet hit, his jump is finished. For this reason you are urging him over and over to get *height off the board*. The triple jumper, however, faces a different problem. When he lands in both the "hop" phase and the "step" phase he must still have enough momentum to complete a good third phase or long jump. He must therefore be coached to avoid trying for height off the take-off board. He must concentrate upon unrestricted momentum through the first two phases. If he gets much height off the take-off board, his entrance into the step phase of the event is going to be hindered because the jolt of his landing will block forward drive. Some indeed come to a near dead stop and their succeeding phases are far too weak to result in a worthwhile total triple jump.

I am convinced that progress in the triple jump in the United States, except in a few isolated instances, is likely to be rather slow and gradual. Rapid progress will come only after many more high schools have added it to their track programs. I am just as firmly convinced, however, that when it does become a widely contested event on the high school level there will be just as outstanding performances in the triple jump as in the long jump or high jump. Some individuals who begin the triple jump after they reach college or when they enter A.A.U. competition will continue to surprise us by world class performances, but when the United States high school track coaches begin to concentrate upon this event and study its techniques there will be dramatic improvement. Although competition in the triple jump at the high school level is in its infancy, there has already been remarkable improvement in the event. See Figure 46.

If you are a high school coach faced with the necessity of developing triple jumpers for the first time, there are certain basic points that you must recognize and certain basic types of practice that you must adopt. One of these points I have already emphasized: the triple jump demands more speed forward than lift upward. If you are working with a converted long jumper, you will have to concentrate upon changing his action off the board. Secondly, if you want to help the boy prepare himself for his best effort, you must convince him of the importance of strengthening his abdominal muscles and of developing strength in his so-called weak leg. Correct motivation of triple jumpers cannot ignore either the forward momentum off the board or the development of the weak leg of the jumper.

A friend of mine, an Olympic triple jumper himself, emphasized to me that the preparation of the triple jumper demanded a great deal of deter-

Figure 46

SCHMIDT OF POLAND WINS OLYMPIC TRIPLE JUMP.

mination and some suffering from the boy who was anxious to be among the best. If your candidate for the triple jump is not willing to face the ordeal of sore, tight leg muscles as he strengthens his weak leg for this event, he will never be outstanding. You must set up a program for the triple jumper that stresses hops *on the weak leg* from one end of the football field to the other. The yardage markers will serve as guide lines for the boy in his workouts. Though at first he may find a succession of hops or steps from his weak leg for *half* the length of the field an agonizing effort, he will find that as weeks go on he is able to continue the effort for the full length of the field. The principle of overload for development is of great importance here.

It would be rather poor coaching for any man to attempt to bring along a triple jumper without insisting that he spend a great deal of time developing leg strength, but it would be equally poor coaching to overlook the importance of rhythm in the over-all effort of a triple jumper. No doubt many coaches have heard of the rhythm pattern that the athlete is trying to achieve in the three phases of his event. It is a fact that the coach can actually listen to his triple jumper in action and be certain whether the jump is a good one or a poor one. He does not actually have to see his man in action to determine whether his jump is successful. The clue to the success or failure of the jump lies in the second phase of the triple jump. The closer the rhythm of each phase is to *regular,* the more likely it is that the jump is a good one. The coach can actually turn his back upon the jumper and listen for what he seeks.

With beginners and others who are having trouble getting distance, the fault often lies in the step phase of the action. If the sound that the coach hears is a *long-short-long* combination, he can be sure that his jumper is not getting the distance that he should from the step phase of his event. All good triple jumpers are trying hard to get full step action. The nearer the jumper comes to achieving this, the more regular will be the sound of the three phases of the action. See Figures 46a, 46b and 46c.

Figure 46a

SANEEV OF RUSSIA WINS 1968 OLYMPIC TRIPLE JUMP.

Photo by Don Wilkinson

Figure 46b

PRUDENCIO OF BRAZIL—TRIPLE JUMP.

Figure 46c

WALKER OF U.S.A.—TRIPLE JUMP.

It is important for the coach also to watch the jumper's knee carefully. In the hop take-off, the athlete must be reminded that the knee of the take-off leg should not go beyond thigh height when the thigh is parallel to the ground. In the step flight, the step knee should be held in front all the way while the take-off leg is brought forward with the knee *under the hip* to help keep the body *up*. Just before the jump landing, the athlete must be trying to bring both knees through and to shoot his feet forward to get maximum distance. In working with triple jumpers, the coach should try to observe the knee action by taking a position to the side. At other times he should watch the jumper from in front to determine that he moves along a straight line and does not sway from side to side. If the coach notices such movement from side to side, he should have his jumper move his take-off leg more under his center.

More than any other event, triple jumping puts a demand upon the strength of the weak leg. Since one phase of the action must be performed from the weak leg, the coach should insist upon the boy's working to strengthen both legs. One of the easiest ways to help the triple jumper get this strength of both legs and at the same time incorporate other aspects of his event is to have him practice the long jump with take-offs first from one foot, then from the other. If he shows serious weakness in his take-off from one leg, have him concentrate on many take-offs from the weak leg.

Often beginners have trouble with the hop because they fail to get the knee up high. The coach can assist the athlete in this phase of his event by having him practice on the football field, using a series of hops down half the field, emphasizing the point of getting the knee *up* on each hop. If the athlete should prove unable to handle a series of hops for the 60 yards, let him try a lesser distance, then walk slowly for about 30 yards and start another series of hops, covering the distance to the back of the other end zone. As he progresses and his legs gain strength, have him increase the distance until he is able to cover the full 120 yards without becoming exhausted.

Another aid to the triple jumper that the coach can use is to have him do continuous steps, using alternate legs, but, as in the hop practice, getting the knee of the free leg *up high* and *holding* it there as long as possible.

Any coach will help his triple jump candidates progress by insisting upon their doing many sprint repetitions of 40-50-60 yards. He can assist them a great deal by having them work often on running a series of three low hurdles. He should realize also that most of our leading triple jumpers today are working with weight training regularly.

You must also urge him to build up as much approach speed as possible and to more literally "run off the board" but then to land in such balance that he will be over his landing foot, *still* with enough forward drive to give him a *long step phase*. Only in the third phase of the triple jump does the jumper become a "long jumper," trying *then* for height to accomplish what the long jumper tries.

Since the triple jump take-off has so great a bearing upon the over-all success of the effort, you will need to work hard on this phase if you want your triple jumper to make progress. After making it clear to the athlete that he is to drive *forward* off the board rather than upward, you should next stress the point that the knee of the free leg should not be raised beyond the point where the thigh is parallel to the ground. The knee of the take-off leg should be brought through with the leg flexed, *not straight*. At the same time, the free leg should be moved backward, relaxed. You must convince the boy that the free leg should *not* be *swung* back or reaction will be spoiled. Emphasize that the *knee* of the take-off leg should be held up as long as possible. These are critical points and must be observed if your triple jumper is to make real progress.

You should next make clear to your triple jumper that the hop landing and the step take-off should combine. Remind your jumper that he must relax just as he lands in order to absorb the shock. His arms should be at his side and his hips relaxed. The beginning of the step take-off is the next critical phase. Stress the point that your jumper must begin the step take-off by swinging his rear leg *up* and through *from behind*. Remind your triple jumper that he must use his arms vigorously to assist his lift in the step take-off. Have him try both common methods to determine which is better suited for him. He may either bring both arms up with his elbows out or have one arm extended in front and the other behind his body.

It is highly important that you urge your jumper to relax and float through the air in the step phase of the event. He will need to hold the knee in front all the way and because this requires strong abdominals and hip flexors, you will need to work long and hard with him to develop these through proper exercising and weight training.

Next, observe the action of the take-off leg in the step phase. Be sure that the boy brings the leg forward with the knee under the hip. This helps greatly in keeping the body up. Remember that poor action in the step phase is the trouble with most weak triple jumpers. The jumper must hold the float position in the step as long as possible. Just before landing, he must swing both arms behind him. You must insist upon this use of the arms because it helps to fight the forward rotation resulting from the angular momentum in the step take-off.

Then, at the take-off, to enter the final phase of the triple jump, the athlete must be sure to swing *both arms* vigorously upward, trying for *height*. Because the triple jumper is likely to have so little momentum left, he will be wise to use the "hang" style of jump rather than the hitch kick used by so many long jumpers. The two-arms swing mentioned above helps the jumper get into good "hang" position. He must be taught to hold that position as long as possible, and just before landing to swing both knees through and to shoot his feet forward. Remind him that he no longer needs to land on both feet but may, if he wishes, land on one.

Some of the Russian coaches tell of using a method of developing leg strength in their triple jumpers and long jumpers indoors also. They describe a set of strong wooden boxes placed one in front of the other so that the athlete springs off the floor and lands on his take-off foot on the box, then on the floor and immediately up on the next box. The procedure can involve a series of hop actions or a sequence of hop and step actions so that emphasis can be placed upon development of either leg or both (Figure 47).

STARTING WORK WITH HAMMER THROWERS

Though the hammer throw can be a dangerous event, it is actually no more dangerous than the javelin throw or, for that matter, the discus

Figure 47

THIS PICTURE ILLUSTRATES A PRACTICE FOR LEG DEVELOPMENT IN THE TRIPLE JUMP, WHICH RUSSIANS WORK ON GREATLY. HOP TO BOX, STEP TO FLOOR, JUMP TO ANOTHER BOX, ETC.

throw. The latter, thrown when the athlete's hands are sweating or when the discus is slightly wet, is often less controllable than the hammer. The carelessness of onlookers or of other athletes in the throwing area is usually far more at fault than the thrower when injuries occur. I have seen plenty of evidence for that statement. To me, this seems a rather weak excuse for not allowing the event in high school meets in so many of our states. I think it is time that we stopped excluding events for such excuses as our officials' or coaches' failure to clear areas in which the various implements are to be thrown. It seems to me that it is about time we stop expecting the little state of Rhode Island to supply most of the hammer throwers entering colleges with sound knowledge of their event. Even at the college level, most of our hammer throwers still come from the New England colleges (who get them from Rhode Island high schools), and from an area in California in which Harold Connolly and his friends have been doing all the ground work.

The coach who is starting the development of a hammer thrower needs first of all to get him accustomed to the turns. He needs to help him to get the feel of heel and toe action in the turns with the hips countering the pull of the hammer as he spins. Actually, the athlete will find that if he is turning properly and the hammer is being countered by his hips, he will not be pivoting high on his toes but on the outer edge of his pivoting foot. Before long the shoe on that foot will begin to show signs of excessive wear. Although some hammer coaches do not like the method, I feel that there is some merit in having the beginner train with a hammer that has a shorter wire than that required in meets. For the early stages of his development, he will get the feeling of better control of the hammer and can concentrate upon correct form in the turns. At this stage of the thrower's development, I think that he should be doing a great deal of practice on the turns *without throwing*.

In recent years, hammer throwers have been recognizing the importance of the wind-up in the over-all process of throwing. They have been making great efforts in the wind-up, to get the hammer moving in the plane in which they will be trying to move it in the turns that follow. For a long time, not much attention was given to this phase of the throw.

Just as weight training has contributed greatly to the effectiveness of our shot putters, discus throwers and javelin throwers, it has become recognized as a vital part of the training for throwing the hammer. No wise coach will neglect weight training in the development of any boy aspiring to be a good hammer thrower.

The coach should realize that the weight training program that he sets up for his hammer thrower must take into account the development of leg strength. Even though the athlete may be a high school youth who is throwing the 12-pound hammer, the strength needed in the legs to enable him to counter the hammer with his hips is great. The ability of the thrower to "sit" and, in a sense, "hang" from the hammer is determined to a great extent by the strength of his legs. See Figure 48.

Photo by Don Wilkinson

Figure 48
NARCESSIAN, RHODE ISLAND
UNIVERSITY—HAMMER AT NCAA
MEET, PROVO, UTAH.

In recent conversations with Bob Backus, a man who has done a tremendous amount of study in the relationship of weight training to weight throwing, I found that he disagrees with those who reject the use of "full squats" in working with heavy weights. The argument often advanced is that no actions in track and field utilize full, deep knee bends but only partial flexing as in the shot, discus, jumps, javelin throw, and hammer throw. An added objection to the deep knee bends is the claim that there is danger to the knees in using heavy weights in these full bends. Bob contends that proper instruction in the bends and the use of protective guards will minimize the danger to knees. His main point, and one which makes a great deal of sense to me, is that using the heavy weights with only partial or half squats is defeating one of the principles of weight training. That is that the exercise should involve full range of motion to develop flexibility. The feeling now of many who have made a study of the weights is that failure to go through the full range of motion in the deep knee bends with heavy weights actually can be responsible for *lack* of flexibility, the very thing that induced coaches earlier to discourage the deep knee bends. This change in attitude toward the use of full bends with heavy weights may be news to many coaches, but it is a practice with many of our best weight men today.

With many beginning hammer throwers, the coach will observe the tendency to try to counter the weight of the hammer with the shoulders and arms. The thrower will actually be leaning away from the hammer with the upper part of his body or remaining very straight and stiff from the waist upward as he turns. If the coach will study our best throwers in action or look carefully at sequence pictures of these throwers, he should notice immediately that there is a slight bend forward from the waist to permit a wider sweep of the hammer, while the countering of the hammer's pull is done with the hips.

Another phase of beginning hammer throwing which the coach should stress is the employment of a wide stance at the start and the shifting of the body weight to the left early in each swing as the thrower tries to get speed for entry into the turns. Unless the beginner learns to get proper spread of the feet, he will find that he is very easily pulled off balance.

When working with the thrower in his delivery of the hammer, the coach should stress the need of having both knees slightly bent to allow the legs to do their powerful lifting along with the rest of the body as the hammer is given its final, explosive impetus (Figure 49).

Photo by Don Wilkinson

Figure 49

NARCESSIAN, RHODE ISLAND UNIVERSITY—HAMMER DELIVERY
AT NCAA MEET, PROVO, UTAH.

There is obviously much more to the development of hammer throwers than the few points that I have touched upon here. These are intended only as a few coaching pointers. The coach who wants to delve deeply into hammer-throwing techniques should get hold of Harold Connolly's book on the event. Few have ever made so complete a study of the event as Connolly has. It is my hope that others who have made a deep study of the weight events will soon get out books revealing the results of their analysis of these events. Studies like Dick Ganslen's in the pole vault and Harold Connolly's in the hammer throw along with Geoffrey Dyson's great book on mechanics of athletics should be only the beginning of specific studies made in individual events.

SOME THOUGHTS ABOUT THE STEEPLECHASE

Here is another event that gets far too little attention except in Olympic years. Even though some college meets are beginning to include it, there is still a great deal of work to be done in preparing athletes for the steeplechase. Don't get me wrong here; I am not about to urge all coaches to incorporate the event in their dual meets. Most coaches of track and field have to spread themselves so thinly now that they need 36-hour days to accomplish what they are trying to do. The steeplechase, however, is another one of those specialties like the hammer throw and the decathlon. It demands a certain type of athlete who is willing to work endlessly to combine a series of techniques for proficiency in an over-all event.

When the coach starts to look around for information about training an athlete for the steeplechase, he is likely to find that most of what has been written deals with the clearance of the water jump (Figure 50). It is true that there are some rather amusing misconceptions about the technique to be used over this particular barrier, but this is far from the only important consideration in the event. The very fact that the steeplechase is a race contested over 3000 meters is of great importance. The fact that along the route there are more real hurdles than water jumps to contend with is another point to remember. We have, therefore, an event which requires a combination of the endurance of the distance runner, hurdling efficiency, and some knowledge of how to clear the water jump effectively. If we assess the event realistically, we must admit that emphasis must be placed first upon the development of endurance, second upon the improvement of hurdle technique, and then upon the perfection of the water jump. It is true that weaknesses in the last two phases can affect the first, but failure to train for endurance is likely to be far more disastrous than weaknesses in hurdling or water jumping.

Perhaps we should think of our best steeplechase prospect as a boy who has speed enough to run a fast mile, strength enough to run a strong three miles, is tall enough to do fairly well in a 400-meter hurdle race, and has determination enough to resemble a decathlon man. The event is truly a most demanding one. What the steeplechaser really faces is approximately a two-mile race during which he must clear 28 hurdles three feet high and

Figure 50

GASTON ROELANTS LEADS THE 1964 OLYMPIC STEEPLECHASE FIELD.

7 water jumps or, if the full two-mile distance is being used, he must take 32 hurdles and 8 water jumps. He faces the water jump as the fourth obstacle each lap. That means the mighty interesting total of 40 obstacles to be cleared in the course of running two miles. When we realize that runners are breaking nine minutes for the 3000-meter steeplechase, we get some idea of how fast the event is being run.

Using the distance, hurdle, water jump relationship as a guide for preparing the athlete mentally and physically for the race, we can figure out a reasonable training schedule combining time for endurance training, practice in 400-meter hurdling, and work on form in the water jump. The necessity for a strong background of distance training is certainly obvious. Cross country running and the related training is mighty important in the preparation of a good steeplechase man. But the coach should not overlook the value of *height* in a good prospect. The very short runner, though he may have good two-mile times, is somewhat handicapped in his efforts in the steeplechase. He is in the same boat as the short man trying to become a high hurdler. He can do it, but he will always be at a slight disadvantage against the rangy two miler who is converted to a steeplechase runner.

I feel that the coach can then best help his runner by having him work quite frequently over the 400-meter hurdles. It is true that the distances between hurdles in the steeplechase are not the same as those in the 400-meter event, but the hurdles are the same height and do assist the steeplechase runner to keep some regularity of stride length even over the 78 meters or the 80 yards between hurdles and water jumps in the 3000-meter or the two-mile event. You have only to watch inexperienced steeplechase runners breaking stride to get in two or three short steps to gather for the clearance to realize how many seconds are being lost in this manner. The steeplechaser is actually a "long distance hurdler." It seems to me to make just as much sense to have him conscious of stride consistency as it does to have the 400-meter hurdler so. Some coaches belittle the importance of good hurdle form in the steeplechase. I am not one of them. I fail to see how any coach or prospective steeplechase runner can shrug off the fact that from 28 to 32 hurdles face the competitor. Even a few tenths of a second saved in the approach and clearance at each hurdle can be an appreciable time advantage, but good hurdle clearance can do even more than that for the steeplechaser. One of the big advantages of good hurdle clearance is in its getting the athlete back on the ground in good balance, thus enabling him to get into full stride quickly. I believe that most steeplechase runners should pay more attention to learning good hurdling form than they do.

In connection with the steeplechase, much more has probably been said about the water jump than it really deserves. Because it is so different from any other phase of a track or field event, it has drawn all sorts of comments and led to some rather interesting studies. Looked at realistically, however, what the runner really faces is the clearance of seven or eight hurdles in an unorthodox hurdling manner and landing each time in water while coming off the obstacle. Concern has been voiced about the effect of the cold water upon the legs of the steeplechaser and the possibility of muscles tightening as a result. Some attention has been given to the advisability of attempting to clear the entire water hole and landing upon the dry terrain just across the water as the Olympic winner did. Other coaches have wondered about the possibility of clearing the hurdle in regular hurdling form and attempting to continue in running stride through the water after landing.

What actual timing has shown to be the fastest and most acceptable method of taking the water jump is that of springing from the ground to land on the wide hurdle cross piece in such a manner as to get a powerful forward thrust from the foot pushing off the cross piece. The steeplechaser then lands on the opposite foot in the very shallow area of the water hole and takes his next step on dry land. Attention has to be given to the avoidance of landing on the hurdle in too upright a position, thus causing a slight halt on the landing and lessening the forward drive off the hurdle and forcing the runner to take a complete stride in the water hole. There can be little doubt that running in water will cut the speed of the runner, but it has also been shown that attempting to clear the water completely is difficult and usually results in the athlete's landing close to edge of the water rather badly off balance, and occasionally even toppling backward into the water. Time thus may be lost rather than gained. A look at the construction of the water hazard will soon indicate to the coach that the water becomes gradually shallower at the end farthest from the hurdle. The steeplechaser will therefore meet with comparatively little water resistance if he gets a strong forward push off the cross piece of the hurdle and lands on the opposite foot close to the water's edge. Almost every good steeplechase runner now uses this method of clearing the water hazard. Unless you are blessed with a steeplechase runner who is tall and extremely strong legged, you will do well to accept the same method for your runner. Perhaps one thing you could do to help the boy is to have him practice running in slightly less than knee level water at the seashore, if this is possible for him.

PREPARING THE DECATHLON MAN

For years it was quite possible to question a dozen track coaches and find that only one or two of them could tell you what events are included in a decathlon. Even today you may find a surprisingly large number of coaches who cannot list the events contested. Even fewer coaches will be found with a knowledge of how the decathlon is scored. But suddenly coaches are beginning to find in their squads a boy or two who express an interest in the decathlon. Some of us are discovering that we have to take a closer look at the decathlon and its scoring. Furthermore, we are finding out that we are being forced to evaluate decathlon prospects to determine whether they do have any real promise in the very demanding event.

The question quickly arises: Is this the event for the athlete who is the "jack-of-all-trades"and "master-of-none?" The answer to that question had better be that he needs to be "master" of several if he is to get very far in the decathlon. Next the coach might ask whether it would be wise to look for a man who is strong in several field events and work with him to improve his running events and hurdling, or to find an athlete who shows outstanding running ability and try to develop him in the field events. The only sensible answer seems to be that the coach must remember that in good competition, the decathlon man is going to have to average about 700 points per event to be in contention. If he is thinking of his athlete as a possible future Olympic prospect, the coach must see in him possibilities for an average of over 800 points per event. Of course, if the coach is thinking in terms of the competition within a league, he may see that an average of 600 points will bring his athlete a championship in the decathlon. Even a 500-point average will bring results in some competition. See Figure 51.

Photo by Don Wilkinson

Figure 51

TOOMEY WINNING THE DECATHLON 400 METER RUN IN 1968 OLYMPICS.

It is interesting to study some of our best decathlon men, especially those who have won Olympic gold medals. I think that much can be learned from such a study. If the coach were asked what was Rafer Johnson's outstanding event, he might find that difficult to answer. The same might be true if he were asked what event was Bob Mathias's best. He would probably know that Bob Richards in the decathlon could amass many points in the pole vault, but he would be hard pressed to tell you what C. K. Yang's outstanding event was. Is there any real clue to the outstanding decathlon prospect? I am going to try to answer that and I do so with full knowledge that I am going to get plenty of opposition from coaches who disagree. Honestly, I welcome the disagreement because I feel that the decathlon has more room for improvement than most coaches realize.

Assuming that I had a tall, strong, dedicated athlete, what event would I consider the key to his possibilities in the decathlon? Would I consider any single event the key to his ability in the decathlon? My answer would be that *I would be extremely interested in his ability as a high hurdler.* Most coaches are aware that the outstanding high hurdler has basic sprint speed. Many are aware that the good high hurdler is often a very fine quarter miler. Others know that the good high hurdler is usually a fine long jumper and quite often a very good high jumper. I might point out that such an athlete is a strong-legged boy who because of his very speed can get distance in the shot put. His speed is valuable in his pole vault approach, and his willingness to attack the high hurdles at full speed is an indication that the pole vault will not be too great a challenge to him. If he has basic speed and strength, he can be given work that will give him the endurance for the 1500-meter run. The one event that may be the weak link in his competition may well be the javelin throw. The coordination that a high hurdler has, coupled with his speed and balance, can surmount the problems of discus throwing. There is no substitute for a fine throwing arm in the javelin. If by some miracle your fine high hurdler has a good throwing arm along with his speed and coordination, you may have a decathlon prospect of real promise. The arm strength that he shows in the javelin throw is of value in the pole vault. The coordination that he shows in high hurdling is vital in discus throwing. The leg strength that he shows in the sprints is of great importance in the long jump and the high jump. You might be surprised sometimes if you checked some of the possibilities of your strong sprinters in the shot put and even in the high jump, but with all of the characteristics mentioned above, the athlete is not a good decathlon prospect unless he shows a willingness to punish himself and an extra measure of determination. What many coaches and athletes overlook is the fact that the ten events that compose the decathlon are made exhausting by the very time limits within which they must be contested. They do not call the Olympic decathlon winner the world's greatest athlete for nothing.

INDEX

A

Adverse conditions, 159-168 (*see also* Conditions, adverse)
Alternate press, 125
Alternate, use, 90-96 (*see also* Relay racing)
Altitude, high, 83
Anticipation, psychology of, 176-177
Approach in jumping, 127-129 (*see also* Jumpers)
Attacks of record, planning, 153-154
Attention, individual, 150-151
Audio-visual aids, 13

B

Backus, Bob, 206
Bannister, Roger, 82
Baton, 89 (*see also* Relay racing)
"Blind" passes, 91
Boston Globe, 126
Bowerman, 78

C

Championship, prepping team, 175-186 (*see also* Prepping team for championship)
Chinning, 125
Clark, Ron, 67, 72
Classroom teaching, 13
Clean and press, 125
Clearance, bar, 127

Climate, extreme, 83
Comfort, psychology, 117
Conditions, adverse:
hurdling against strong wind, 164-165
indoor racing conditions, 165-166
ordinary precautions not enough, 161-162
practicing in rain, 162-164
relay passes for problem areas, 165
some seeming trivia, 166-168
value of modern investigations, 159-161
varying approaches, 162
Coordination in relay racing, 89-90 (*see also* Relay racing)
Cousy, Bob, 61
Cromwell, Dean, 12
Cross bar, 126-127, 134
Cross piece, 49
Cureton, Dr. Thomas, 70, 81, 82

D

Danek, 108
Decathlon man:
ability as high hurdler, 213
best men, 212
events contested, 211
javelin throw, 213
points per event, 212
scoring, 211
speed and balance, 213
Delaney, Ron, 84
Dintiman, Dr. George B., 24, 25

Discus thrower's exercises, 125
Distance and middle distance runners, 60-87 (see also Middle distance and distance runners)
Distance runners, improvement, 179-181
Dodds, Gil, 169, 170
Doherty, Ken, 11, 12, 78
Drive, inner, 153
Dyson, Geoffrey, 25, 160, 208

E

Eastman, George, 95
Extended meet, 184-186

F

Fartlek work, 77, 78, 79
Finish at tape:
   arms driven backward, 39
   banked turn indoors, 40
   Newton's Third Law, 39
   run on the curve, 39
   run-through style, 39
   running the turn at full speed, 40
   split-second timing, 37
   thrust finish, 39
   thrust of chest, 37
   tight finishes, 37
   turn outdoors, 40
Force application, 137
Fouling, what it reveals, 112-114
440-yard run, 64
Frank Ryan Enterprises, 35
"Free space," 93-94
Fuchs, Jim, 107
"Full squats," 206

G

Gaines, Billy, 20
Ganslen, Dick, 208
Gerschler, Dr. Woldemar, 77
Gerschler-Reindel Law, 77, 78
Greene, Charlie, 21
Guild, Dr. Warren, 77
Gun jumper, 29-33 (see also Sprinters)

H

Half milers, 66-70
Hammer throwing:
   Backus, Bob, 206

Hammer throwing (cont.)
   balance, 207
   California, 205
   Connolly, Harold, 208
   dangerous event, 204
   delivery, 207
   development of leg strength, 205-206
   "full squats," 206
   "hang," 206
   Rhode Island, 205
   "sit," 206
   turns without throwing, 205
   weight training, 205
   wide stance at start, 207
   wind-up, 205
Hand-on-hip reception, 91, 94
"Hang," 203, 206
Hayes, Bob, 20
Heel protectors, plastic, 51
Height off board, 198
Hemery, Dave, 58
Henry, Franklin M., 62, 63
High jumping, 126-127
Hines, Jim, 21
"Holism," 11, 78
"Hop," 198, 203
"Hurdle intervals," 54
Hurdlers, developing:
   boy who balks, 46-47
      intermediate height, 46, 47
      low hurdle, 46
      shortened distance, 47
      wind at back, 47
   confidence for three steps, 49-53
      coming off first hurdle, 51
      do three things well, 52
      good hurdlers, 51-52
      head well forward, 50
      knee of trailing leg, 51
      landing on heel, 50
      plastic heel protectors, 51
      practice over one hurdle, 50
      rhythm of strides, 49
      small faults, 52
      third hurdle, 53
      trailing leg after clearing, 51
   correcting hurdle jumper, 48-49
      difficulty with trailing leg, 49
      disclosing poor prospect, 48
      full speed approaches, 49
      loops or movies, 49
      loose cross piece, 49
      padded hurdle, 49

Hurdlers, developing:
  correcting hurdle jumper (*cont.*)
    stand near wall, 48
    tight hips, 48
  flexibility exercises, 48
    common hurdle, 48
    loosen hips, 48
    stretching, 48
    use trailing exercise, 48
  intermediate hurdles, 56-58
  keying on head position, 59
  overcome fear, 45-46
    "dive" action at full speed, 46
    move hurdle closer, 46
  over-distance hurdling, 54-55
    avoid overdoing, 55
    endurance, 54
    "hurdle intervals," 54
    shuttle hurdle relay, 55
    sprint interval training, 54
  spend time on one hurdle, 47
  wind conditions, 53-54
  working the low hurdler, 55-56
Hurdles, improvement in, 178-179

I

Igloi, 67, 68, 78
Improvement:
  distance runners, 179-181
  events, 178
  hurdles, 178-179
  sprinters, 179
"Increasing Running Speed," 24
Individual attention, 150-151
Indoor racing conditions, 165-166
"Inner drive," 153
Inside pass, 91, 94, 96

J

Javelin thrower:
  coaching, 117-123
  exercises, 125
Jerome, Harry, 21
Jumpers:
  approach, 127-129
    adjustments, 128
    angle, 127
    bar clearance, 127
    consistency, 128
    indecision, 127
    take-off areas, 129
    tentative take-off mark, 127

Jumpers (*cont.*)
  coaching help for long jumpers, 134
  cross bar, 126-127, 134
  developing confidence, 127
  difficulties, 131
  getting height off board, 135-137
    body weight, 135-136
    flat placement of foot, 136
    force applied, 137
    length of force application, 137
    shortening last two strides, 135
    take-off leg slightly bent, 135
  high jumping, 126-127
  landing, 137-138
  speed and long jumping, 134-135
  take-off, 129-130
  tension in opponents, 131-134
    cross bar, 134
    "on" and "off" days, 131-132
    short person near uprights, 134
    wide margins, 132

K

Kidd, 84
Koufax, Sandy, 61

L

Larrabee, 171
Lateral raises, 125
Lift, extra:
  fear of pulled muscle, 34
  full speed *and then some,* 33
  groups of muscles, 34
  half and three-quarter speeds, 34
  mechanics of sprinting, 34-36 (*see also*
    Sprinters)
  mind and body, 34
  sustained sprinting effort, 34
  two purposes, 33
  untapped speed reserves, 33
  vigorous but relaxed action, 33
  watching sprinter's head, 34
Lindgren, Gerry, 72, 74
Lonely Breed, 72
Long jumpers, 134-135, 197, 203
Long-short-long combination, 200
Long step phase, 202
Loops, 49
Losing streak, breaking:
  assessing team's chances, 188-189
  big effort, 191-193

Losing streak, breaking (*cont.*)
  hiding your strength, 190-191
  meet tactics, 193-195
  planning workouts, 189-190
  problem of new morale, 187-188
Lydiard, 66, 67, 78

M

Matson, Randy, 106
Mays, Willie, 61
Mechanics of Athletics, 25, 160,
Meet, extended, 184-186
Meet rules, 183-184
Middle distance and distance runners:
  beginner, 60-61
    super-stars, 61
    sustained speed, 61
    temperament, 61
  dangers of stress, 64
  developing mediocre talent, 62-63
  440-yard run, 64
  half milers, 66-70
    background in cross-country, 70
    build-up of boy, 68
    changing systems, 70
    consider individuals, 69
    demands of track schedules, 67
    endurance, 66
    high speed repetitions, 68
    immediate and distant goals, 67-69
    oxygen debt, 69
    training schedules, 67
  lead in distance racing, 87
  quarter miler, 61-62
    endurance, 62
    speed workouts, 62
    sprint type racing, 62
    sustained speed, 62
  racing tactics for distance runners, 85-
    86
  racing tactics in 880, 70-72
  special considerations, 65-66
  stimulating the star, 63
  working with distance runners, 72-85
    cross country running, 77
    extremes in climate, 83
    fartlek work, 77, 78, 79
    fatigue and hard exercise, 80
    goals set in advance, 80
    gradual stress, 81
    group or team training, 75
    high altitude, 83

Middle distance and distance runners:
  working with distance runners (*cont.*)
    "Holism," 78
    individual workout schedule, 77
    individual's part in group workout,
      79
    interval training, 77
    key points of work schedule, 84-85
    "keyed up" athlete, 82
    motivate toward achievement, 74
    oxygen debt and fatigue, 82
    pace, 77
    pain, 72, 73, 74
    pulse rate, 78, 80-81
    recovery phase of training, 78
    training schedule, 74
    win athlete's respect, 75
Mills, Billy, 171
Modern Training for Running, 11
Morale, 187-188
Movies, 13, 49
Muscle pull:
  pressure bandage, 41
  rejection of immobility, 41
  spikes in shoes, 42
  sprinter's shoes, 41
  taping, 41
  "waiting for another pull," 41

O

O'Brien, Parry, 107, 108
Ogilvie, Dr. Bruce, 114, 153
Opponent's psychology:
  early stages of events, 173-174
  faith in own ability, 173
  racing strategy as motivation, 171-173
  respect opponent's ability, 170-171
  some fear is not folly, 171
Opposition, checking and using, 154
Oral correction of weaknesses, 13
Owens, Jessie, 20
Oxygen debt, 69

P

Packing a weak event, 181
Paddock, Charlie, 37
Personal sequence shots, 13
Pole vaulter, fibre glass:
  confidence for the wait, 142-143
    athlete's belief in coach, 143
    bend creates problem, 143
    correcting fallacies, 142

Pole vaulter, fibre glass (*cont.*)
  direction of pole bend, 143-144
    center of gravity, 144
    "compound pendulum," 144
    energy stored in pole, 144
    left or back, 143-144
    pull up on pole, 144
    timing leg lift, 144
    vaulter low on pole, 144
    vertical drive, 144
  matching pole and vaulter, 146
  observations and recommendations, 149
  placing the uprights, 145-146
    head in the rock back, 146
    rules guarantee rights, 145
    snap of neck, 146
  rock back, 144-145
  weight training, 146-148
  wind conditions and approach, 145
Precautions, 161-162
Prepping team for championship:
  extended meet, 184-186
  importance of seeding, 181-182
  improvement in hurdles, 178-179
  improvement of distance runners, 179-181
  improvements in events, 178
  let some events alone, 181
  making use of meet rules, 183-184
  packing a weak event, 181
  psychology of anticipation, 176-177
  significance of seedings, 182
  sprinters show limited improvement, 179
  value of early planning, 177
  "winning on paper," 176
Press, 125
Pressure bandage, 41
Problem Athletes and How to Handle Them, 114, 153
Problems, preparation for, 159-168 (*see also* Conditions, adverse)
Psychology of opponent, 169-174 (*see also* Opponent's psychology)
Pull-overs, 125
Pulled muscle, 40-42 (*see also* Muscle pull)
Pulse rate, 78, 80-81

Q

Quarter miler, 61-62

R

Racing conditions, indoor, 165-166
Rain, practicing, 162-164
Raises, lateral, 125
Record breaker:
  checking and using opposition, 154
  considerations for future, 155-156
  individual attention, 150-151
  planning attacks of record, 153-154
  playing up athlete's strengths, 154-155
  significance of "inner drive," 153
  star as team aid, 151
  tension and outstanding athlete, 155
  using status symbol, 151-153
  distance and medley, 100-102
  individual and team effort, 88-89
  placing men for effect, 96-97
    advantage of vocal signal, 96
    danger with visual signal, 97
    danger with vocal signal, 96
    starting signal, 96
    vocal and visual signals, 96
  putting pressure on opponents, 102-104
    contribution of protective time, 103
    cutting down lead gradually, 103
    ten-yard zone marked off, 104
    weak man at anchor, 103
    weak man second, 103
  "take charge" man, 98-100
    baton exchanges at top speed, 98
    dropping batons, 98
    experiments, 98-100
    illustrating exchange point, 98
    vocal and visual signals, 98
  use of alternate, 90-96
    advantages of right-to-left pass, 95
    "blind" passes, 91
    conventional left to right pass, 91, 95
    dangers of inside pass, 96
    differences in exchanges, 91
    "free space," 93-94
    frequent use of *inside pass,* 94
    hand-on-hip reception, 91, 94
    "inside" pass, 91, 94-95
    maximum speed during exchange, 94
    passing too soon, 90
    reasons for use of passes, 93
    types of passes, 91
    variations of exchanges, 91
    worst problem in sprint relay, 94
  working for coordination, 89-90
    baton, 89

Record breaker:
working for coordination (*cont.*)
lead-off man, 89
perfecting baton passing, 90
sprinters in front, 89
where to deliver baton, 90
Right-to-left pass, 95
Rock back, 144-145
Rope climbing, 125
Rules, meet, 183-184
"Run off the board," 202
Russell, Bill, 61
Ryder, Jack, 170
Ryun, Jim, 13, 61, 67, 68, 72, 73, 74, 75, 79, 159

S

Sales, Bob, 126
San Romani, Archie Jr., 13
Scholastic Coach, 24
Schul, Bob, 171
Seedings, 181-182
Selye, Dr. Hans, 11, 81, 82
"Sit," 206
Sit-ups, 125
Slides, 13
Smith, Tommy, 20
Snell, Peter, 67, 68, 74
Special events:
beginning triple jumpers, 197-204
decathlon man, 211-213
hammer throwers, 204-208
steeplechase, 208-211
Spikes in shoes, 42
Sprecher, P., 78
Sprinters:
after a muscle pull, 40-42 (*see also* Muscle pull)
demanding greater effort, 22
differences in potential, 19
extra lift, 33-36 (*see also* Lift, extra)
finishing tactics, 37-40 (*see also* Finish at tape)
flexibility exercises, 24
mechanics, 34-36
ankle flexibility, 35
facial muscles, 35
finish of the dash, 36
high knee action, 35
muscle strongest under stretch, 35
Newton's Third Law, 35
runner's body angle, 35
splay-footed action, 35

Sprinters:
mechanics (*cont.*)
time of day, 36
vigorous arm action, 35
what *should* be done, 34
mismotivation, 22
natural talent, 20
reacting to gun jumper, 29-33
competitive 15-yard dash, 31
concentrating upon *GOING,* 29
first motion upward, 31
full stride, 31-33
lack of concentration, 30
rising sharply as gun sounds, 30
readiness for starting, 29
recognition of potential, 19
relaxation, 22
running at four-fifths speed, 21
show limited improvement, 179
"something held back," 22
starting, 27-28
bunch start, 28
medium elongated start, 28
position is highly individual, 27
science of *human motion,* 28
theories of physicists, 28
supplement sprint training, 24
timing drive for tape, 36-37
accept pain, 37
endurance, 36
planned move, 36
timing the starter, 29
weight training, 24-27
body mechanics, 25
heavy weights with slow lifts, 26
laws of motion, 25
light dumbbells in runner's hands, 26
light weights with fast lifts, 26
muscular endurance and strength, 26
Newton's Second Law, 25
psychological lift, 27
Squats, 125
Star as a team aid, 151
Status symbol, 151-153 (*see also* Record breaker)
Steeplechase:
distance training, 210
endless work, 208
endurance, 208
fast, 209
figuring training schedule, 209
400-meter hurdles, 210
hurdle technique, 208

Steeplechase (*cont.*)
  real hurdles, 208
  specialty, 208
  water jump, 208, 210-211
"Step" phase in triple jump, 198, 200, 203
Supine press, 125

T

"Take charge" man, 98-100 (*see also* Relay racing)
Take-off in jumping, 129-130
Taping, 41
Tensions of individual, handling, 114-116
Thomas, John, 126
Thompson, 167
Timmons, Bob, 13, 79
Triple jumper:
  abdominal and hip flexor, 203
  abdominal muscles, 198
  arms, 203
  avoid *height off board,* 198
  both arms, 203, 204
  continuous steps, 202
  demand upon weak leg, 202
  determination and suffering, 199
  development of weak leg, 198
  40-50-60 yards, 202
  "hang" style of jump, 203
  high school level, 198
  hop landing, 203
  "hop" phase, 198
  knee up high, 202
  long jumpers, 197, 203
  long-short-long combination, 200
  long step phase, 202
  principle of overload, 199
  rhythm pattern, 200
  "run off the board," 202
  single landing, 198
  speed forward, 198
  "step" phase, 198, 200, 203
  step take-off, 203
  strong wooden boxes, 204
  three low hurdles, 202
  United States, 198
  unrestricted momentum, 198
  watch jumper's knee, 201, 203
  weak foot, 197
  wrong foot hits board, 197
Tutko, Dr. Thomas A., 114, 153

U

Uprights, placing, 145-146

V

Vaulter, fibre glass pole, 139-149 (*see also* Pole vaulter, fibre glass)
Visual signals, 97
Vocal signals, 96

W

Walters, Coach Tracy, 72
Water jump, 208, 210-211
Weak event, packing, 181
Weight exercises, 125
Weight men:
  build-up of implement speed, 107-108
    crossover leading to delivery, 108
    O'Brien style, 108
    rhythmic action at high speed, 108
  coaching javelin throwers, 117-123
  concentration of effort, 106-107
    clichés about good loser, 107
    developing great strength, 107
    emphasis upon winning, 107
    faulty start, 107
    multiple trials allowed, 107
    perfection of technique, 107
  exercises, 125
  handling implements, 105-106
    interest in weight events, 106
    javelin throw, 105-106
    speed and coordination, 106
    weight training programs, 106
  handling individual's tensions, 114-116
  problem of balance, 109-111
    coaching shot put, 111
    gradual perfection of techniques, 111
    inability to handle speed, 109
    inadequate speed, 109
    moving in balance, 109
    principles, 111
    speed across circle, 109
    speed uncontrolled, 109
    throw on balance, 109
    use of hips, 109
  psychology of comfort, 117
  securing controlled speed, 108-109
    beginning shot putter, 108-109
    outward signs of effort, 108
    rhythmic build-up of power, 108
  weight training as motivation, 123-125

Weight men (*cont.*)
  what fouling reveals, 112-114
    balance, 112, 113
    head, 112
    left foot, 113
    need of concentration, 113
    rotation of hips, 112
    speed in straight line, 112
  as motivation, 123-125
  sprinters, 24-27 (*see also* Sprinters)
Wilt, Fred, 20, 78

Wind:
  at hurdler's back, 47
  conditions, 53-54
  hurdling against, 164-165
Wind-up, 205
Winter, Bud, 35
Workouts, planning, 189-190

Z

Zatopek, 70, 73, 74, 75, 84